THE
FINAL
COUNTDOWN

DANIEL'S
SEVENTY SEVENS
AND THE
FINAL DECREE
EVERYONE MISSED

Surely the Lord God does nothing, unless He reveals
His secret to His servants the prophets.
(Amos 3:7)

Books by Best-Selling Author
James Harman

The Open Door[1]
Salvation of the Soul[1]
Daniel's Prophecies Unsealed[1,2]
Come Away My Beloved
Calling All Overcomers
Overcomers' Guide to the Kingdom
The Kingdom
The Coming Spiritual Earthquake[1]
The Blessed Hope

Books by Award Winning Author
Dr. Christian Widener

Witnessing The End
The Temple Revealed[3]

1) Amazon #1 New Release Best Seller.
2) Amazon Top 10 Best Selling Book under Christian Old Testament
   Commentaries from 2018 to 2023.
3) First Place 2022 Christain Indie Award Winner that showed the
true location of the Jewish Temple. Josh McDowell wrote in the
foreword to **The Temple Revealed**: "the implications of his findings
are nothing short of world-changing."

THE
FINAL
COUNTDOWN

DANIEL'S
SEVENTY SEVENS
AND THE
FINAL DECREE
EVERYONE MISSED

James T. Harman

**Prophecy
Countdown
Publications**

The Final Countdown

Copyright © 2023, James T. Harman
Prophecy Countdown Publications, LLC
P.O. Box 941612
Maitland, FL 32794
www.ProphecyCountdown.com

ISBN: 978-1-7332995-7-2 (Paperback)
ISBN: 978-1-7332995-4-1 (eBook)
ISBN: 978-1-7332995-5-8 (Audio)

Scripture is from the King James Version (KJV) unless noted otherwise.

Scripture quotations from the Amplified Bible (AMP) Copyright © 1987, by The Lockman Foundation. Used by permission.

Scripture quotations from The Holy Bible, Berean Study Bible, (BSB) Copyright © 2016, 2020 by Bible Hub All Rights Reserved Worldwide. www.biblehub.com

Scripture quotations from The Holy Bible, English Standard Version (ESV) Copyright © 2001 by Crossway, a publishing ministry of Good News Publishers. Used by permission. All rights reserved.

Scripture quotations marked (NASB) are from the New American Standard Bible Copyright © 1995 by the Lockman Foundation, La Habra, CA. All rights reserved.

Scripture quotations from the Thomson Chain Reference Bible, New International Version (NIV), Copyright 1973, 1978, and 1984 by International Bible Society.

Scripture quotations from the New King James Version (NKJV) Copyright © 2013, by Holman Bible Publishers. All rights reserved.

Scripture quotations from the Holy Bible, New Living Translation (NLT), Copyright © 1996, 2004, 2015 by Tyndale House Foundation. Used by permission of Tyndale House Publishers, Inc., Carol Stream, Illinois 60188. All rights reserved.

Numerical references to selected words in the text of Scripture are from James H. Strong Dictionaries of the Hebrew and Greek words.

The Young's Literal Translation (YLT) was by Robert Young, who believed in a strictly literal translation of God's Word and this version is in the public domain.

Certain words such as Kingdom and Judgement Seat are capitalized to emphasize their importance, but not in accordance with Traditional fashion.

Throughout this book, bibliographical references may be provided in the comments on selected texts with the commentator's last name along with the page numbers (in parenthesis) for the references cited.

Credit and Copyright for pictures inside this book:

Page 24 – Suleiman the Magnificent: Portrait of Suleiman the Magnificent by Titian, c.1530 https://commons.wikimedia.org/wiki/File:EmperorSuleiman.jpg

Page 62 – *The Bride* by Dorothy Spaulding – For a copy call: 803-278-3618

Back Cover image of the Dome of the Spirits and the Dome of the Rock on the Temple Mount by Christian Widener, www.WitnessingTheEnd.com

Dedication

To my beautiful daughter, Jennifer
Who has been told by all the doctors
They cannot offer her any hope.
Hang on for just a little while
Because our Lord and Saviour
Will be returning much sooner
Than most people think.
If the message in this writing
Is correct, we will be
Dancing with Jesus
Very soon!

THE WATCHMAN

(Pastors, Teachers, Evangelists and Saints)
Ezekiel the Watchman for Israel
Again the word of the LORD came to me, saying,

2 "Son of man, speak to your people and tell them: 'Suppose I bring the sword against a land, and the people of that land choose a man from among them, appointing him as their watchman, 3 and he sees the sword coming against that land and blows the ram's horn to warn the people.

4 Then if anyone hears the sound of the horn but fails to heed the warning, and the sword comes and takes him away, his blood will be on his own head. 5 Since he heard the sound of the horn but failed to heed the warning, his blood will be on his own head. If he had heeded the warning, he would have saved his life.

6 But if the watchman sees the sword coming and fails to blow the horn to warn the people, and the sword comes and takes away a life, then that one will be taken away in his iniquity, but I will hold the watchman accountable" (Ezekiel 33:2-6 – BSB).

Prologue

Back in 1986, my wife Cindy wanted to place a bumper sticker on our car that read: *Jesus Is Coming Soon*. I remember telling her not to do it because we don't know when He is coming. Being the humble, dutiful wife that she is, she did not argue with me but decided to pray for me.

Cindy's prayers were soon answered when Edgar Wisenant appeared on the scene with his books: ***On Borrowed Time*** and ***The Rapture: Rosh-Hash-Ana 1988 And 88 Reasons Why***. After reading Edgar's books I humbly apologized to my wife and asked her to please forgive me for being so ignorant. I spent the next two years pouring over Edgar's entire voluminous research notes and after his failed prediction I began intently studying the subject of prophecy. Prophecy Countdown was born as Cindy and I began writing our monthly newsletter to a growing number of hungry believers desiring to be looking for the Blessed Hope (Titus 2:11-13) of our Lord's return.

In the spring of 2022, we republished Lyn Mize's wonderful book: ***The Open Door***. We believe his excellent resource can be instrumental in helping believers qualify to become part of the called, and chosen, and faithful (Rev 17:14) who will be granted the magnificent opportunity to reign and rule with Jesus when He returns very soon. The same week that it was introduced on Amazon we found another important new book entitled: ***Witnessing The End – Daniel's Seventy Sevens and the Final Decree Everyone Missed***. Written by Dr. Christian Widener, who has uncovered one of the final pieces to the puzzle, which will help us discover when Christ may return.

Regardless of what you know about Bible Prophecy, his book will totally shock you. If you have an open mind and a teachable heart his book can help you realize how close our Lord's return really is. This book: ***The Final Countdown*** is being produced to help condense his findings and summarize the essential details to reach more of the Church with his vital message.

A key to understanding the prophecy in Daniel 9 is to realize that the Seventy Weeks were fulfilled at Christ's first coming. This is known as the Messianic View and it is well summarized in Chapter 4 and Appendix 4 of our book: *Daniel's Prophecies Unsealed*. Excerpts of this material are included in Appendix 1 of this book.

The Seventy Weeks vision given to Daniel is a picture of God's ultimate plan to bring forgiveness to the entire world through a new covenant (see Jeremiah 31:31-37). From the time of the early church, Daniel's vision has always been applied to the Messiah fulfilling the six purposes given in Daniel 9:24. Many prominent scholars have applied the fulfillment of these six purposes to the Messiah (Barnes, Carroll, Hengstenberg, Hewitt, Mauro and Young to name a few).

In Dr. Widener's award-winning first book *The Temple Revealed*, he uncovered where the Temple was located on the Temple Mount. While doing his research he learned that the city of Jerusalem and its walls had been rebuilt a *second time* in the period from 1537 to 1541 by Sultan Suleiman. This was in fulfillment of a prophecy by Isaiah: *"Foreigners will rebuild your walls, and their kings will serve you"* (Isaiah 60:10).

He then discovered that Suleiman's decrees had been etched on stone plaques providing us with a permanent record. By connecting the dots back to the prophecy in Daniel he has been able to *unseal* the final key to the book of Daniel: **God foreknew and ordained another decree that everyone missed.** The shocking discovery is that God planned a SECOND fulfillment of this magnificent prophecy!

If this remarkable finding is correct and God has planned a Second fulfillment of Daniel's Seventy Weeks, then we are living in the final days and, as Christian's title appropriately suggests, we are indeed *Witnessing The End!*

The purpose of this book is to distill this important message to help people understand where we are in God's prophetic time and to thereby inspire the reader to get ready to meet Jesus sometime this decade.

Table of Contents

Is God a Date Setter?

- God set a date for the flood and revealed it to righteous Noah (Genesis 7:11).
- God set a date for the destruction of Sodom and revealed it to Abraham and Lot (Genesis 18, 19).
- God set a date for Isaac to be born and told it to Sarah and Abraham (Genesis 17:21).
- God set a date for Israel to come out of Egypt and revealed it centuries before he instructed Moses to do so (Genesis 15:13; Gal 3:14-17; Exodus 12:40).
- God set a date for the cattle of Egypt to die and told Moses and Pharaoh (Exodus 12:40).
- God set a date for the defeat of Moab and revealed it to Isaiah earlier (Isaiah 16:14).
- God set a date for the end of the Babylonian captivity and revealed it to Jeremiah decades in advance (Jeremiah 25:11).
- God set a date for the fall of Babylon and told it to Jeremiah and revealed it to Daniel (Jer 27:4-7; Daniel 5:25-30).
- God set a date for the first coming of Jesus Christ and told it to Daniel, Mary, Joseph, and Simeon in advance (Daniel 9; Mat 1:18-25; Luke 2:26-32).

Surely the Lord God does nothing, unless He reveals His secret to His servants the prophets.
(Amos 3:7 – NKJV)

*"When the Spirit of truth comes, he will guide you into all the truth, for he will not speak on his own authority, but whatever he hears he will speak, and he will declare to you **the things that are to come.**"*
(John 16:16 – ESV)

Foreword

God has richly blessed the prophetic ministry of James T. Harman. Jim has the gift of being a modern-day prophet as he proclaims the Good News of Jesus Christ with power. He is a Spirit-filled and Spirit-led teacher of the Bible.

Everyone will give thanks for the blessings of hearing the proclamations of this warm-hearted evangelist. He teaches the inspired Word, he exalts the living Christ, and he honors the Church of the living God.

I can recommend Brother Harman after reading this wonderful book and knowing that he will teach the Word with compassion and will manifest his concern for lost people.

I also recommend his prophetic teachings to any congregation that would like to hear more on the Second Coming of our Lord and the signs that appear before He returns.

I know that Brother Harman's new book titled: *The Final Countdown* will inspire many and reach people that have never trusted Christ as their personal Saviour.

Brother Harman strongly believes that we are nearing the end of this present age and with that view, I wholeheartedly agree.

In His Wonderful Name,

Reverend Colin H. Deal
End Time News

Church minister of 47 years and bestselling author of numerous books and booklets (with over 500,000 in print), and a monthly newsletter concerning the end of this present age and the return of Christ (please see the Bibliography for his mailing address).

This book contains a message that has unsealed the final key to the book of Daniel. Dr. Christian Widener has uncovered a precious treasure that has been hidden for over 2,500 years.

*Although I heard, I did not understand. Then I said, "My lord, what shall be the end of these things?" And he said, "Go your way, Daniel, for **the words are closed up and sealed till the time of the end.** Many shall be purified, made white, and refined, but the wicked shall do wickedly; and none of the wicked shall understand, **but the wise shall understand**.*
(Daniel 12:8-10 – NKJV)

Preface

When Jesus came the first time, the religious leaders should have been able to determine the time. They had been instructed by the angel Gabriel to "**know and understand**" the timing in Daniel 9:25. Had they studied and applied Daniel's prophecy, they would have known that their Messiah was present! Because they failed to discern these things, they were admonished by the Lord.

> *Whenever you see a cloud rising out of the west, immediately you say, 'A shower is coming'; and so it is. And when you see the south wind blow, you say, 'There will be hot weather'; and there is. Hypocrites! You can discern the face of the sky and of the earth, **but how is it you do not discern this time?** (Luke 12:54-56)

Day and Hour

To ensure that we are not rebuked by Jesus, let's take a better look at what the Word of God has to say about knowing the timing. The most widely used verse people quote when they want to prove that we are not to know when Jesus is returning is found in Matthew:

> *But of that day and hour knoweth no man, no, not the angels of heaven, but my Father only* (Matthew 24:36 – KJV).

What most people fail to remember; however, is the preceding verse: *"Heaven and earth shall **pass away**, but my words shall not pass away"* (Matthew 24:35 – KJV). The day and hour that no one knew about when Jesus spoke those words were when heaven and earth will pass away at the end of the 1,000-year Millennium. The timing of when this will occur is found in Revelation 21:1: *Now I saw a new heaven and a new earth, for the first heaven and the first earth had passed away.*

The reason that this time is not known is found in Revelation 20:3, which says Satan is let out of the bottomless pit at the end of 1,000 years for: "a LITTLE SEASON." No one but God knows how long Satan will have to deceive the nations at that time.

Thief in The Night

The teaching that the wise and faithful will know and the unfaithful will not know was taught to us by Paul:

Now, brothers...about times and dates we do not need to write to you, for you know very well that the day of the Lord will come like a THIEF in the night. While people are saying, 'Peace and safety,' destruction will come on them suddenly, as labor pains on a pregnant woman, and they will not escape.
(1Thessalonians 5:1-3 – NIV).

Most people stop reading at the end of the third verse to try to prove their point that the Lord is going to come as a thief. He is coming like a thief, but to whom is He coming as a thief? Notice what Paul says in the fourth verse: *"But you, brothers, are not in darkness so that this day should surprise you like a THIEF."*

Paul is saying that the Lord's coming should not surprise the Christian (brother). While the rest of the world will be surprised like a thief, the Christian should not be surprised.

This confirms what Jesus taught in His parables. The wise and faithful steward will be READY, WAITING and WATCHING for Him when He comes for them. The unfaithful and foolish servant will not be looking for Him and they will be taken by surprise.

The act of *"watching"* is serious business with our Lord. If we fail to continue diligently watching, Revelation 3:3 gives us a fair warning:

*Remember therefore how thou hast received and heard, and hold fast, and repent. If therefore **thou shalt not watch**, I will **come on thee as a thief**, and thou **shalt not know** what hour I will come upon thee* (Revelation 3:3 – KJV).

Those who are not *"watching"* will be taken by surprise since a thief comes unannounced. The wise and faithful followers of Jesus; however, will be *"watching"* for Him and they will not be surprised.

The message in this book is that Jesus is returning very soon. If you have not been watching, begin *"watching"* today before it is too late! Jesus is coming very soon!

Introduction

[5]By faith Enoch was *taken up so that he did not see death*: "He could not be found, *because God had taken him away*." For before he was taken, *he was commended as one who pleased God.* [6]And without faith it is impossible to please God, because anyone who approaches Him must believe that He exists and that *He rewards those who earnestly seek Him*. (Hebrews 11:5-6 – BSB)

Enoch was Noah's great grandfather who is mentioned in the great hall of fame chapter on faith (Hebrews 11). Enoch was the first person to experience the rapture, which is described in Genesis: [24]*Enoch walked with God, and then he was no more, because God had taken him away* (Genesis 5:24 – BSB).

Because Enoch walked with God and he *pleased* Him with the life that he lived, God took him away before the time of the Flood arrived. While the Word of God does not indicate when this event occurred, there is a book entitled: *The Secrets of Enoch*, which records that Enoch was raptured on his birthday, the sixth of Sivan. The sixth of Sivan just happens to be the Feast of Pentecost (Day of Firstfruits). Enoch was born and also raptured on the Feast of Pentecost.

Very little is known about Enoch who was a righteous man who walked with God and pleased Him with the life that he lived. We also know that Enoch preached about the second coming of the Lord and about the coming judgment on those who are ungodly:

[14]Enoch, the seventh from Adam, also prophesied about them:
"Behold, the Lord is coming with myriads of His holy ones
[15]to execute judgment on everyone, and to convict all the ungodly of
every ungodly act of wickedness and every harsh
word spoken against Him by ungodly sinners."
(Jude 14-15 – BSB)

From Enoch's life (as a type-picture), we can surmise that participation in the coming rapture will be for those people of faith who are walking with God, living a life that will be found pleasing to Him.

Those taken in the rapture will also be actively watching for the soon return of the Lord and fervently telling others to get ready before it is too late as Enoch did.

This book contains a message that will not be acknowledged by everyone. Many in the Church will reject it because it goes against the many traditions so prevalent today, particularly about discussing a time for the Lord's return.

Nevertheless, the final piece of the puzzle in the book of Daniel has been found. It was literally hidden in plain sight until Dr. Christian Widener uncovered this treasured gem. His discovery will utterly astound you.

You are about to find out how God used a man named Sultan Suleiman to fulfill a prophecy given to the Prophet Daniel over 2,500 years ago. You will also learn how God utilized former President Donald Trump to help implement His plan for the final countdown in Daniel's prophecy.

More importantly, you will come to understand that our Lord Jesus Christ actually taught on the subject of the Rapture on two different occasions. Understanding His teachings will have a sobering effect on many.

Finally, once you are able to grasp the important truths expounded in this book, you will want to share this information with everyone you care about. You will be impelled to tell others that Jesus Christ is getting ready to return and of their need to be living a life that will be found pleasing in His sight just like Enoch.

Hang on to your hats because you are about to go on an exciting journey that will totally change your life!

Chapter 1

THE END IS NEAR

Is Jesus Christ Your Lord and Saviour?

A s noted by Lyn Mize in the introduction to his book *The Open Door*, "there is one place in the Bible that states what a person must do in order to be saved. That verse states very simply the one and only one step for a person to be saved. The verse is as follows:

> Acts 16:31 (KJV) *And they said,* **Believe on the Lord Jesus Christ, and thou shalt be saved,** *and thy house.*

This requirement for salvation could not be any simpler. There is not a step two to God's plan of salvation. There is only one step, and those well-meaning preachers, teachers and authors who add additional steps to God's plan are adding to the Bible. Some tracts give as many as twelve steps for salvation.

Jesus said, "Truly, truly, I say to you, *he who believes in Me has eternal life*" (John 6:47). The Bible has "been written so that you may **believe** that Jesus is the Christ, the Son of God, and that *by believing* you may have life in His name" (John 20:31). You must believe that you are saved by simply believing in Jesus for eternal life (1 Timothy 1:16). We enter heaven through Jesus, who said, "I am the way, and the truth, and the life; no one comes to the Father but *through Me*" (John 14:6). "I am the door; if anyone enters *through Me*, they will be saved" (John 10:9). We are saved *"through Him"* (Romans 5:9).

God the Father has designed a plan by which you can reach heaven. And His Son, Jesus has done all the work necessary in carrying out that plan. All you have to do is simply trust in Jesus alone for eternal life. The salvation that Jesus provides is completely by His marvelous Grace! (Ephesians 2:8-9).

The Final Countdown was written to alert the Church that Jesus Christ is about to return. If you have never believed on the Lord Jesus Christ for your personal salvation, then you should do so right now. As described above, believing on the Lord Jesus Christ is the only requirement for salvation.

If you feel the prompting of the Holy Spirit, please take a moment and turn to the *Special Invitation* section in this book on page 85.

Welcome back! We hope that you have made one of the most important decisions in your life by trusting your personal salvation to our Lord and Saviour Jesus Christ. Now that you have been saved by the precious blood of the Lamb you should ask the Holy Spirit to help you as you read the Bible to learn all that God has for your life.

The next three chapters of this book will discuss how the Prophet Daniel was given an important prophecy that can be found in Daniel 9. This is one of the most debated chapters in the Bible and opinions vary widely as to the correct meaning.

Chapter 2 will show you what is known as the Messianic view of Daniel's Seventy Weeks, which was taught from the time of the early church. This view shows that Daniel's 70 weeks were completed at the time of Christ's first coming.

Chapter 3 will show the astonishing finding by Dr. Christian Widener that a man known as Suleiman the Magnificent was God's instrument to initiate another decree to rebuild the walls of Jerusalem in 1537.

Chapter 4 will show you how Suleiman's decree started the Second Fulfillment of Daniel's 70 weeks. If Dr. Christian Widener's finding is correct, then Jesus will return before this decade is over.

Chapter 5 will show you where the Lord Jesus Christ taught His disciples He will come for His Church in two phases. This important chapter may have a direct impact on when you will get to see our Lord.

Chapter 2

TIMING OF CHRIST'S FIRST COMING

Seventy-Sevens After the First Decree

From the time of the early church, Daniel's 70 Week Prophecy has applied to Jesus Christ being the one to fulfill the prophecy. This was known as the Messianic view and was considered the accepted doctrine from the time of Jerome down through the centuries.

The following are some of the prominent expositors of God's Word who taught that the Seventy Weeks of Daniel applied to our Lord and Savior Jesus Christ and not the Antichrist: Albert Barnes, B.H. Carroll, Ian M. Duguid, A.R. Fausset, Sinclair B. Ferguson, Curtis Hahn, Matthew Henry, E.W. Hengstenberg, Clarence H. Hewitt, Saint Jerome, Philip Mauro, Sir Isaac Newton, J.E.H. Thomson, John Urquhart, Ralph Woodrow and Edward J. Young.

Then in the late 1800's a new contemporary interpretation surfaced, which captivated the masses with a new "tradition" that has become the modern church dogma of today. My original view of eschatology was firmly indoctrinated into believing this new tradition. Being a CPA, I was fascinated by the precision Sir Robert Anderson created in his book: **The Coming Prince**, which is considered the standard volume in the field and followed by most in today's church.

Anderson was a former Chief of Criminal Investigation in Scotland Yard who studied and wrote extensively, particularly on the subject of prophecy. His book gives very detailed and complex calculations which appear to give convincing "proof" that Daniel's prophecy predicted the exact day Christ was crucified. Because of this, Anderson's work has become the "gold standard" for people to go to in the book of Daniel.

The "traditional" teaching of today on the 70th Week of Daniel was developed from a change in the Authorized King James Bible back in 1885. The following is a brief excerpt from Appendix 3 of *Calling All Overcomers*: "This popular church tradition is a relatively new one. Dave Watchman wrote on this subject in an article entitled *The Truth of Daniel 9:27*. He notes that the error began in 1885 when the 'Revised Version' (R.V.) was recommended to be the <u>replacement</u> for the Authorized King James Bible by the so-called 'textual critics' of that Era. He then compares the purified Authorized Version (A.V.) with the corrupted Revised Version (R.V.) which renders Daniel 9:27 falsely. The R.V. "makes" the "he" the Antichrist, compared to the purified A.V. text which declares the "he" to be Jesus Christ:

Authorized King James Bible	The Revised Version of 1885
And <u>he shall confirm the covenant</u> with many for one week: and in the midst of the week he shall cause the sacrifice and the oblation to cease, and for the overspreading of abominations he shall make it desolate, even until the consummation, and that determined shall be poured upon <u>the desolate.</u>	And he shall make a firm covenant with many for one week: and for the half of the week he shall cause the sacrifice and the oblation to cease: and upon the wing of abominations shall come one that maketh desolate; and even unto the consummation, and that determined, shall wrath be poured out upon <u>the desolator.</u>

"...the A.V. says '*and he* (Jesus) *shall confirm* (strengthen) the covenant (referring to the Abrahamic covenant already mentioned in Daniel 9:4 and Genesis 12:1-3) with many for one week (7 years)', whereas the R.V. says 'And "he" (Antichrist) will make a firm covenant (peace) with many for one week (7 years)."

His article goes on to point out that Sir Robert Anderson and C.I. Scofield were close friends who used the false rendering brought out by the Revised Version in their classic works: *The Coming Prince* and the *Scofield Bible*. As time passed, other writers such as Larkin, Ironside, Pentecost, Walvoord, etc. wrote prophetic books that agreed with Sir Robert Anderson's faulty interpretation, which has formed the basis of today's popular teaching.

This changes the entire meaning of Daniel's magnificent vision and distorts the true significance of this important prophecy. Instead of being about the wonderful story of how God sent His Son to provide Israel with an extended period of grace over a period of 490 years, the prophecy becomes a fabricated tale about the Antichrist coming to make a "7-year" peace treaty that is somehow *split off* from the first 483 years that were fulfilled at the time of Christ's first coming. This story has become the modern staple for the church today; blinding everyone from seeing the beautiful story Daniel was given.

Analysis of Anderson's *The Coming Prince*

The basis of most of today's eschatology was arrived at through the influence of Sir Robert Anderson and C.I. Scofield. Anderson's work was based upon three erroneous assumptions: an incorrect starting date, the use of a corrupted version of Scripture, and the manipulation of dates through a faulty mode of reckoning.

Incorrect Starting Date
While Anderson begins his calculation of Daniel's seventy weeks with the correct decree of Artaxerxes' reign, the 20th year of the King did not occur in 445 BC, but in the year 454 BC as discovered by Dr. Floyd Jones (see p. 44 in **Daniel's Prophecies Unsealed**).

Corrupted Scripture
Instead of using the Authorized King James Bible of 1611, Anderson used the corrupted Revised Version of the Bible that came out in 1885. This incorrect rendering replaces Jesus Christ with the Antichrist, thereby changing the entire meaning of Daniel's prophecy. This flawed change has created today's teaching that has permeated most Bibles and books on prophecy. Anderson's work is now a cherished tradition that is dogmatically believed by almost everyone.

Faulty Reckoning
After beginning with an incorrect start date, Anderson used a 360-day lunar year to arrive at his conclusions. Instead, he should have used our normal solar year of 365 days to calculate Daniel's seventy weeks.

Anderson's work has recently come under attack due to his use of a 360-day prophetic year that Hengstenberg has noted was "a mode of reckoning, which was never adopted by the Hebrews, and therefore is so thoroughly destitute of foundation, that we need not stop to prove its incorrectness…"(Hengstenberg, p. 211).

Today's "traditional" teaching has created a faulty scenario where the Church is "Raptured" away before the Antichrist comes to make a 7-year peace treaty with Israel. We find it extremely interesting that the word *Tradition* has a Gematria that totals: 666! In light of the findings in this book, which show the true meaning of Daniel's vision, readers are encouraged to seriously reconsider Anderson's work.

Timeline for Seventy Weeks
The timeline for the Seventy Weeks prophecy can be found on the following page. This timeline has been adjusted from the one shown in **Daniel's Prophecies Unsealed** to reflect Dr. Christian Widener's different starting date.

He used the start date of 457 BC (Decree in the 7th Year of King Artaxerxes) and then moved forward 7 weeks (49 years) and then another 62 weeks (434 years) for a total of 483 years. This comes to 27 AD when Christ began His ministry. We believe His ministry was about 3 ½ years and in the middle of the final 70th week; Jesus was crucified (cut-off). After Christ's death, the Gospel message was preached almost exclusively to the Jewish people until the time recorded in Acts 10. There the Apostle Peter received a supernatural vision and he was sent to the house of Cornelius where he preached the Word of God and the Holy Spirit fell on the Gentiles for the first time; thereby ending the 490 years in approximately 33 AD.

The Seventy Weeks of Daniel were completely fulfilled during the time of Christ's first coming. The marvelous prophecy given to Daniel that is recorded in Daniel 9, was fully completed during Christ's first coming. Please see Appendix 1, which is an excerpt from **Daniel's Prophecies Unsealed**. There you will see all of the details of our original timeline and the changes we have incorporated to reflect portions of Dr. Christian Widener's great book.

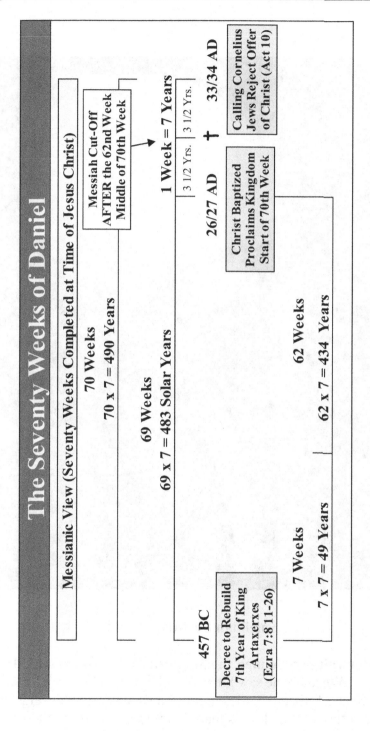

The Seventy Weeks of Daniel

Messianic View (Seventy Weeks Completed at Time of Jesus Christ)

70 Weeks
70 x 7 = 490 Years

Messiah Cut-Off
AFTER the 62nd Week
Middle of 70th Week

69 Weeks
69 x 7 = 483 Solar Years

1 Week = 7 Years

3 1/2 Yrs. | 3 1/2 Yrs.

26/27 AD   33/34 AD

Christ Baptized
Proclaims Kingdom
Start of 70th Week

Calling Cornelius
Jews Reject Offer
of Christ (Act 10)

457 BC

Decree to Rebuild
7th Year of King
Artaxerxes
(Ezra 7:8 11–26)

7 Weeks
7 x 7 = 49 Years

62 Weeks
62 x 7 = 434 Years

Suleiman the Magnificent

Portrait of Suleiman the Magnificent by Titian, c.1530
We know he saw himself as the second Solomon
because he had the title engraved in stone during his reign.
Most of the gates and walls that we see today were rebuilt by him.

Chapter 3

SULEIMAN THE MAGNIFICENT

God's Vessel to Rebuild Jerusalem

O nce the nation of Israel had rejected their Messiah, and God turned His attention to the Gentiles, the seventy weeks (490 years) in Daniel's vision were completed. God then turned His attention to the Gentiles with the conversion of Cornelius.

Desolation of Jerusalem
The Jewish people had been given an extended period of grace of seventy weeks or 490 years. They crucified the Messiah and rejected the message the Apostles brought to save them. To make matters even worse, they continued to offer sacrifices in their Temple, which truly was an abomination in God the Father's eyes after they had rejected the sacrifice of His Son.

As noted by Hengstenberg, "The ancient temple is…changed, on account of the unbelief of the [Jewish] people and the murder of the Messiah, from a house of God into a house of abomination, which must be destroyed" (Hengstenberg, p. 169).

Because of this, God had the Roman armies sweep into Jerusalem to desolate the city and the Temple: *"…and for the overspreading of abominations he shall make it desolate, even until the consummation, and that determined shall be poured upon the desolate"* (Daniel 9:27–KJ).

This shows that the flood of God's wrath against the Jews was because they continued to offer sacrifices in the Temple, which was the abomination that forced Him to send Titus to desolate the city. This desolation will continue until the consummation when the times of the Gentiles are completed.

The vision of the seventy weeks is a magnificent prophecy of God sending His Son to redeem all of mankind. Even though Israel rejected their Messiah, God is not finished with them or with the Holy City of Jerusalem.

From 70 AD until the sixteenth century, the Holy City was in a state of disrepair and ruins. Then in 1517, the Ottomans took control for the next four centuries. Ottoman sultan, Selim took possession of Jerusalem in March of that year, but when he died in 1520, he was survived by his only son, Suleiman. Suleiman was only 25 years old at the time and he found himself the ruler of an empire that stretched from the Balkans to the borders of Persia, from Egypt to the Black Sea.

"In Bagdad, I am the Shah, in Byzantine realms, the Caesar; and in Egypt, the Sultan,' he declared and to these titles he added that of caliph. No wonder the Ottoman courtiers addressed as…emperor, or as one of them wrote, 'the most honoured and respected sovereign the world over.' It is said that **Suleiman dreamed he was visited by the Prophet** who told him that 'to repulse the Infidels,' he must embellish the Sanctuary (Temple Mount) and **rebuild Jerusalem,'** His wife would repeatedly hail him, 'the Solomon of his age.' Suleiman inherited Jerusalem…and believed that his Islamic prestige demanded that he beautify the sanctuaries of Islam…His achievements in Jerusalem were so successful that the Old City today belongs more to him than anyone else."[1] [Emphasis added.]

An overlooked prophecy given by Isaiah tells us:

Foreigners will rebuild your walls, and their kings will serve you (Isaiah 60:10).

Sultan Suleiman was given a dream that he was to rebuild the walls of Jerusalem and that he was to beautify the Temple Mount. Between 1537 and 1541, he undertook the mission that had been given to him in a prophetic dream by 'the Prophet.'

It appears that Suleiman the Magnificent was God's chosen vessel to fulfill Isaiah's prophecy of rebuilding God's Holy City of Jerusalem.

The city of Jerusalem that we see today is mostly the result of the achievements of Sultan Suleiman. As noted by Dr. Christian Widener:

The Decrees Carved in Stone!
"Sultan Suleiman restored many parts of Jerusalem between 1537-1541. His equivalent name in English is literally Solomon, and we know that he saw himself as a second King Solomon because he had the title engraved in stone during his reign…He placed carved stone plaques at many of the specific repairs that he made around the city to document them. But those stone plaques stand as a permanent record of his decrees regarding the restoration of Jerusalem…decrees that are etched in stone."[2]

The Church is indebted to the remarkable findings made by Dr. Christian Widener. In the following chapter of this book, we will present several of his findings from these stone plaques that will give us clues to the timing of Christ's Second Coming.

Daniel's Vision – Pointing to Christ (Cut-off Middle of 70th Week)
We need to remember that the prophecy that was given to Daniel was given to him by the angel Gabriel.

*23) At the **beginning** of your supplications the command went out, and **I have come to tell you**, for you are **greatly beloved**; therefore consider the matter, and **understand the vision**:*
> *24) **Seventy weeks** are determined for your people and for your holy city, to finish the transgression, to make an end of sins, to make reconciliation for iniquity, to bring in everlasting righteousness, to seal up vision and prophecy, and to anoint the Most Holy (Daniel 9:23-24).*

The seventy weeks vision given to Daniel is a picture of God's ultimate plan to bring forgiveness to the entire world through a new covenant (see Jeremiah 31:31-34). In the previous chapter, we saw how the Seventy Weeks of Daniel were completely fulfilled during the time of Christ's first coming.

Daniel's holy vision given by the angel Gabriel pointed to Jesus Christ.

Suleiman's Dream – Points to Antichrist (Middle of 70ᵗʰ Week)
Sultan Suleiman was given a dream by *the Prophet* instructing him to rebuild the walls of Jerusalem. This was to bring about the fulfillment of the prophecy in Isaiah 60:10, with foreigners rebuilding the walls.

God used Suleiman the Magnificent to fulfill His purpose of restoring His Holy City between the years 1537 to 1541. As we will see in the next chapter, Suleiman's dream will be tied to God bringing about the SECOND fulfillment of the Seventy Weeks of Daniel.

But this time it will be pointing to the Antichrist appearing in the middle of the 70ᵗʰ week, with Jesus fulfilling the entire Seventy Weeks at the Second Coming of Christ!

Dual Application To Scripture
The prophecies given in Daniel were given for a dual purpose:

> *Now I have come to make you understand what will happen to*
> *Your people **in the latter days**, for the vision refers to*
> ***Many days yet to come*** (Daniel 10:14).

It is important to understand that the term the *latter days* has a dual meaning. When this was given to Daniel, it referred to the *first coming* of Jesus Christ to announce the kingdom to the Jewish people. But because God foreknew Jesus would be rejected by the Jews, the *latter days* also represents the time of Christ's *second coming*.

Similarly, the prophecy regarding the 70 Weeks also has a dual purpose. From the time of the early church, Daniel's 70 Weeks has applied to Jesus Christ fulfilling the prophecy (Messianic view). God also foreknew that there would be *another decree* to rebuild Jerusalem that He also ordained—pointing to the return of Jesus Christ at His *second coming* to rule and reign in the coming Kingdom.

The following chapter will outline how the decree *everyone missed* is being fulfilled right before our eyes. You will learn how Sultan Suleiman's decree began the Second fulfillment of Daniel's Seventy Weeks, which will be completed before this decade is over.

Chapter 4

TIMING OF CHRIST'S SECOND COMING

The Final Decree Everyone Missed

B ecause of the traditional interpretation that is believed and taught by the majority of Christians alive today, what you are about to discover will totally shock you. Most will immediately reject this new perspective and refuse to genuinely consider it. Changing one's paradigm is extremely difficult; particularly when it goes against everything we have been taught. As Author Bloomfield has said about tradition, "a person once infected is very difficult to reach. It seems as if one simply cannot get through to him."

Practically everyone who studies prophecy is looking for the Antichrist to arrive on the scene to make a 7-year peace treaty with Israel. Then after 3 ½ years, he is to break the treaty and begin his 42 months of persecution (Daniel 7:21, 25, 9:27).

Under this popular traditional teaching, the Rapture will take place before this 7-year treaty is signed and the entire Church will be taken away from the horrible tribulation period.

This author held this view until Marvin Rosenthal wrote his book: *The Pre-Wrath Rapture of the Church*. Attending the same church with Marvin motivated me to be a staunch Berean (Acts 17:11). As a result, the Lord showed me that he is partially correct. However, I also discovered that he missed the first phase of the rapture that Jesus also taught. This important aspect will be discussed in the next chapter.

Blinded By Traditions?
Most who hold to the popular 7-year peace treaty tradition may have been blinded by popular theory. When you think about it, why would Israel enter into a peace treaty that only had a term that lasted 7 years?

What would happen at the end of those 7 years? Would the parties to the treaty go back to their previous state of affairs and begin military operations? It would not make very much sense to enter into a peace treaty that had a fixed limit to its length. When you really think about it, why would anyone enter into such an agreement?

What you are about to read will help explain the passages in Daniel and it will completely change your perspective on where we are in God's prophetic timeline. Daniel's prophecy regarding the 70 Weeks includes a unique verse that specifically mentions the restoration of Jerusalem with *plaza* and *moat*:

> So you are to know and discern that from the issuing of a decree to restore and rebuild Jerusalem until Messiah the Prince there will be seven weeks and sixty-two weeks; *it will be built again, **with plaza and moat**,* even in times of distress. (Daniel 9:25 – NASB)

New Discovery by Dr. Christian Widener

"In verse 25, it says that Jerusalem's restoration will include work at a "plaza and moat." If you read different translations, you will find that they have struggled with the proper meaning of the ancient Hebrew words in English. Some have translated it "streets" and "trench" for example….the word for plaza, *rechob,* was specifically used in Ezra 7:15-19, speaking about the plaza of the temple (i.e., the Temple Mount). It can also mean a wide street area (for a meeting place at a gate or square in the city), but we have a good scriptural tie for associating it with the temple, in this case."

"The word *charuwts* can mean a moat or trench, but a simple trench, such as a large ditch dug in the earth or rock, would not be listed as a structure that needed to be restored. It makes more sense that it was a large, fortified moat. Thus, plaza and moat look like the best translations of those words. Another reason we can be confident that the reference is to a moat is because one of the repairs Suleiman made included an actual moat. It can still be seen today around the Citadel of David, the so-called Tower of David (see photo, at the top of the next page), near the Jaffa Gate inside the Old City."

"The view is from the east side of the tower, looking north, and was taken January 13, 2020.

When the moat was repaired, he embedded a carved stone plaque in the wall to document his work. The part of the moat where the plaque is located was buried in1898, but a photo of it was taken before it was covered over in the expansion of the city.

The photo below was taken by Max van Berehem before it was covered over in the expansion of the city."[172]

"Here is the translation of the stone plaque above:[173]   *The order to* construct this tower for protection of the Islamic walls by his power and duration of his reign, and to dispose of the favouring idols by his force and strength, the One that did Allah especially elected to rule the neck of the Kings in the World, the possessor in chain of the throne of Caliphate, Sultan son of Sultan, son of Sultan, Son of Sultan…"

"It is truly amazing! There is an actual moat within the Old City of Jerusalem and it has a plaque proclaiming its restoration by Suleiman; however, there is no date on this specific plaque…"

"Fortunately, that is not the only plaque I want to show you. Suleiman also extensively repaired the plaza of the temple, and he placed a fountain (*sabil*) and another plaque with an inscription to document its restoration. It not only confirms that the Temple Mount was an area restored by Suleiman, but it also gives us a date for his decree. It is called *Sabil Bab el Atm*, meaning fountain at the Gate of Darkness (see photo, *below* [174])."

174 Sabil Bab el Atm photo by Chris Yunker, November 18, 2007.
175 Photo of Suleiman's decree courtesy of Veit Ullrich, April 2022.

"The translation of the plaque[175] is: *"He has ordered* the construction of this blessed Sabil, our Master, the Sultan, the greatest Sultan and the honourable Hakan, who rules the necks of the nations, the Sultan of the lands of Rum, the Arabs and Persians (ajams), the Sultan Suleyman, son of Sultan Selim Khan, may Allah perpetuate his reign and his sultanate, On the date of Hijra of the Prophet at the beginning of Shaban the blessed in the year 943. And blessings be upon Muhammed and upon his followers."[176]

176 Tütüncü. *Turkish Jerusalem*, 74; In total, Suleiman had nearly three dozen inscriptions documenting his work in Jerusalem between 1536-1541. Within the walls of the city, the oldest is at the *Sabil el Wad*, which is near the *Bab el Kattanin* (Cotton Merchants Gate) of the *Haram al-Sharif* (Temple Mount). It is dated December 14th, 1536. The next oldest one is at another fountain (*sabil*) in the city called, *Sabil Bab el Silsile*, dated January 4, 1537. These dates are all very close. I've highlighted the one that is located on the plaza of the temple (the Temple Mount), since "plaza" is mentioned in verse 25. Either way, we are looking at a decree date that is between December 14th, 1536, and January 23rd, 1537."

"The plaque Suleiman had placed there is located at the north end of the Temple Mount about fifteen meters south of the Gate of Darkness (*Bab el Atm*), as shown in the diagram below. It is dated "the beginning of Shaban 943." The date given by this plaque converts to a modern date ranging from between the 13th to the 23rd of January, 1537 on our Gregorian calendar.[177] That gives us a verifiable date range from which to begin counting 483 years forward. ...if you count 483 years from 1537 that brings us to the year 2020!"[3]

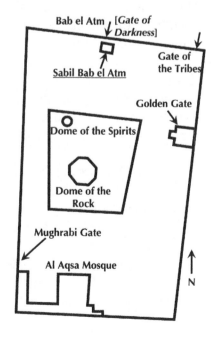

Has The Final Countdown Begun?

Could it really be true? Has another 70th Week of Daniel actually begun without anyone realizing it? Have we entered into the final week and has the Final Countdown begun?

In the last chapter, we discovered how Sultan Suleiman was God's chosen vessel to fulfill the prophecy in Isaiah 60:10, that foreigners would rebuild the walls of Jerusalem. Now we see that Suleiman documented his work with over three dozen inscriptions etched in stone! And then we find that Suleiman placed his decree on the Temple Mount in the year 1537 (around January).

> So you are to know and discern that from the issuing of a decree to restore and rebuild Jerusalem until Messiah the Prince there will be seven weeks and sixty-two weeks; *it will be built again, **with plaza and moat**,* even in times of distress (Daniel 9:25 – NASB).

If we multiply 69 weeks (7 weeks + 62 weeks) times 7, we get 483 years. And if we go forward 483 years from 1537, we arrive at 2020!

This means that Suleiman's decree in 1537, began the Second fulfillment of Daniel's Seventy-week prophecy. The final 70th Week of Daniel's prophecy began in 2020.

If this is true then there should be some evidence. Remember in the last chapter we came to realize there may be a dual rendering of Daniel's prophecy with the Antichrist confirming a peace treaty. Let's see what took place in 2020 regarding a possible covenant.

The Confirmation of the Covenant With Many

Dr. Christian Widener reminds us:
"First, we had an Israel-Palestine peace plan, sponsored by President Donald Trump and formally published on January 28th, 2020.[180] The plan was released almost exactly 483 years after these inscriptions. Then later the same year, some of the gulf Arab states began making peace with Israel under the Abraham Accords.[181]

The first agreements were officially signed on the White House lawn on September 15, 2020. They were initially signed by UAE, Bahrain, Morocco, and Sudan, and other nations are also expected to adopt and sign these agreements. Hence, a new era of peace began in the region in 2020, as some key Arab states expressed their recognition of Israel and their interest in a broad-range collaboration to mutually benefit their countries.

Because Daniel's prophesied *"confirmation of the covenant"* will begin a final period of seven years, many expect there will be a formal peace treaty for a precise period of seven years. However, a seven-year time limit on the agreement is not explicit in the text. **The Bible may say seven years because that is all the time that is left**. Consequently, an agreement at the start of the tribulation would be *de facto* a seven-year agreement. Furthermore, by naming these peace deals with Israel as the ***"Abraham Accords,"*** we are being shown that the "confirmation of the covenant" has been satisfied simply in the naming of the peace agreements" [Emphasis added].[4]

Incredibly, the world may have witnessed the beginning of the final seven years for the Second fulfillment of Daniel's Seventy Weeks without even knowing it! Trump's peace plan and the Abraham Accords with *the many* nations could be the prophetic implementation of God's final plan. (Please see Appendix 2, 3 and 4 for more details).

Chart – Second Fulfillment of The Seventy Weeks of Daniel
The chart that can be found on the next page summarizes what you have just read into a picture of where we may be in God's final timeline. This chart will probably upset you if you don't really want the Lord to come. If you are like me and you can't wait for Jesus to return, this will be exciting news that it may not be very much longer until we can get to be with our Lord.

The danger for all of us is to stubbornly defend what we have always believed because we are convinced it is true. But we could be wrong about some things so we always need to have a teachable spirit and open mind when it comes to the Word of God.

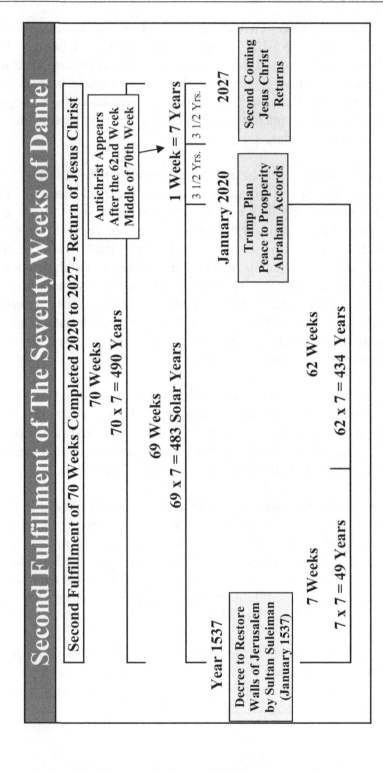

Second Fulfillment of The Seventy Weeks of Daniel

Second Fulfillment of 70 Weeks Completed 2020 to 2027 - Return of Jesus Christ

70 Weeks

70 x 7 = 490 Years

69 Weeks

69 x 7 = 483 Solar Years

1 Week = 7 Years

Antichrist Appears
After the 62nd Week
Middle of 70th Week

| 3 1/2 Yrs. | 3 1/2 Yrs. |

January 2020

2027

Trump Plan
Peace to Prosperity
Abraham Accords

Second Coming
Jesus Christ
Returns

Year 1537

Decree to Restore
Walls of Jerusalem
by Sultan Suleiman
(January 1537)

7 Weeks

7 x 7 = 49 Years

62 Weeks

62 x 7 = 434 Years

Chapter 5

THE TIMING OF THE RAPTURE

The Two Phases Jesus Taught

The timing of the rapture is one of the most controversial issues in the Church today. The traditional Pretribulation Rapture is the most popular view, but popularity should not be the measure of Scriptural truth. As alluded to in the previous chapter, this author held the Pretribulation view until Marvin Rosenthal introduced his Pre-Wrath Rapture position. We believe his view may be partially correct; however, we also think that he is incorrect in thinking that God will not remove any believers before the start of the *great tribulation*.

Phased Rapture Position
We have come to believe that the Bible teaches that the Rapture will take place in two distinct phases where the Lord will remove His Firstfruit believers at the beginning followed by the removal of the remaining believers in the Main Harvest before God pours out His wrath. It is important to point out that Jesus taught the doctrine of a "phased" Rapture of believers in both the earlier and later parts of His ministry. First, in the Sermon on the Mount, Jesus taught His disciples to pray for deliverance from the Tribulation period (Matthew 6:13). At the very end of His ministry when He gives His famous discourse on the Mount of Olives, He also instructs His followers to always pray for escape from the same Tribulation period (Luke 21:34-36).

*34) And take heed to yourselves, lest at anytime your hearts be overcharged with surfeiting, and drunkenness, and cares of this life, and so that day come upon you unawares. 35) For as a snare shall it come on all them that dwell on the face of the whole earth. 36) **Watch ye therefore, and <u>pray always</u>, that ye may be <u>accounted worthy</u> to <u>escape</u> all these things that shall come to pass, and to stand before the Son of man*** (Luke 21:34-36 – KJV).

Jesus chose to teach His disciples this principle of a "phased" Rapture because there is a way to escape the *great tribulation.* The first time on the Mount of Beatitudes when He gave the famous "Lord's prayer," He tells us: ***"And do not lead us into temptation**[3986] **but deliver us from the evil one*** (Matthew 6:13 – NIV). The Greek word for temptation is #3986 (peirasmos) which is the precise same term that Jesus uses in His promise to the Church of Philadelphia:

> Since you have kept my command ("word" – KJ) to endure patiently, *I will also keep you from the hour of trial*[3986] that is going to come upon the whole world to test those who live on the earth (Revelation 3:10 – NIV).

In other words, in the Lord's prayer, Jesus is telling us that we should be praying for God to deliver us from the coming trial of the Antichrist (evil one). This is the promise given to the Church of Philadelphia and it is also the same prayer mentioned above in His instructions on the Mount of Olives (*pray always to be accounted worthy to escape*).

Please notice that both times were on a "***Mount,***" both times He taught this ***privately*** to His disciples, and both times He included important instructions in a ***prayer*** for His disciples to follow. Jesus would not have taught us to pray to escape the coming Tribulation if it were not possible to do so. So while escape is possible, please notice that it is also very conditional. We need to *be accounted worthy to escape* (Luke 21:36) and we need to be *found keeping His word* (Revelation 3:10) to escape the coming tribulation period.

The faithful Philadelphian believer has the ears to hear and the heart to understand this teaching while most of the Church prefers to follow the Traditions of man (Colossians 2:8). The faithful, overcomer heeds the Lord's advice and continually *prays for deliverance* from the coming Tribulation period.

This teaching is not a new idea but was taught by many great men of God in the Philadelphia church age. Men like J. Hudson Taylor, Dr. A.B. Simpson, John Wilkison, Joseph A. Seiss, and Ray Brubaker. To learn more about this teaching please see *The Open Door* by Lyn Mize or download any of our free books at: www.ProphecyCountdown.com.

Now that we see that there is a way to escape the coming tribulation period, we need to see how this fits in with the fact that the tribulation will not be for the traditional period of 7 years as we have been taught.

We believe that the *great tribulation* is only 3 ½ years long and the traditional Pre-Trib, Mid-Trib, and Post-Trib Rapture positions can now be modified using the Phased Rapture approach with the faithful Firstfruit believers (accounted worthy) taken at the beginning followed by the rapture of the Main Harvest believers (lukewarm) at the end.

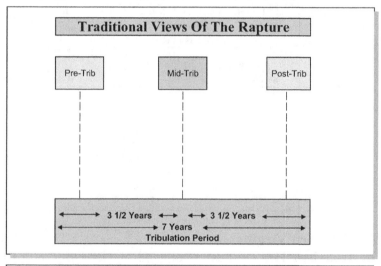

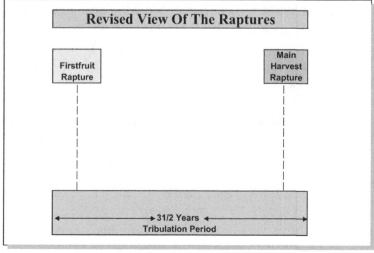

We need to remember that if Sultan Suleiman's decree in 1537, began the Second fulfillment of Daniel's Seventy-week prophecy then the final 70th Week began in 2020. This means that the Antichrist is due to appear very soon. Depending upon when in 2020 the final 7 years began, the mid-point could be anywhere between 2023 and 2024. The purpose of this book is not to set an exact date, but to alert the reader to the fact that time is very short and everyone needs to be preparing their hearts to meet Jesus today, while there is still time.

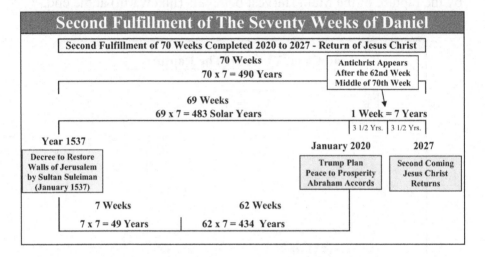

Parable of the Ten Virgins

The Great God of Heaven has announced in His Holy Word that a grand wedding is about to take place. Mankind's time on this earth is about up, and the Bridegroom is getting ready to return for His bride. Are you part of the bride of Christ? Will you be ready when Jesus returns? Who is it that is invited to the wedding banquet? It is those described in Revelation 19:7 and 9:

> ...For the wedding of the Lamb has come, and his bride has made herself ready...Then the angel said to me, "Write: Blessed are those who are invited to the wedding supper of the Lamb!" And he added "These are the true words of God (Revelation 19:7,9 – NIV).

Notice that the above verse says, *"The bride made herself ready..."* How did she make herself ready?

> And to her it was granted to be arrayed in fine linen, clean
> and bright, for the *fine linen is the* **righteous acts** *of the saints*
> (Revelation 19:8 – NKJV).

The bride made herself ready for the wedding by obtaining her fine
linen. This was her reward for the righteous life that she lived. The
original Greek confirms that this fine linen is not the righteousness
that is imputed to every believer in Christ but represents the
righteous acts or the righteous living of the believer (conduct, acts,
and deeds) following their salvation. This same teaching was
confirmed for us by Jesus when He taught about the ten virgins:

> 1) Then the kingdom of heaven shall be likened to ten virgins
> who took their lamps and went out to meet the bridegroom. 2)
> Now five of them were wise, and five of them were foolish. Those
> who were foolish took their lamps and took no oil with them, 4)
> but the wise took oil in their vessels with their lamps. 5) But
> while the bridegroom was delayed, they all slumbered and slept.
> 6) And at midnight a cry was heard: 'Behold, the bridegroom is
> coming; go out to meet him!' 7) Then all those virgins arose and
> trimmed their lamps. 8) And the foolish said to the wise, 'Give us
> some of your oil, for our lamps, are going out.' 9) But the
> wise answered, saying, 'No, lest there should not be enough for
> us and you; but go rather to those who sell, and buy for
> yourselves.' 10) And while they went to buy, the bridegroom
> came, and those who were ready went in with him to the
> wedding; and the door was shut (Matthew 25:1-10 – NKJV).

Here we see that only the five wise virgins who were ready went
to be with their Bridegroom. All 10 virgins were Christians because
all did possess their oil, which represents the Holy Spirit who was
given to each of them upon their conversion. The 5 foolish virgins,
however, did not carry along the extra measure of oil that the 5 wise
virgins carried in their jars. The 5 wise virgins were ready because
they were obedient to the Word of God, which commands us to be
"filled with the Spirit" (Ephesians 5:18). Because the 5 wise virgins
were filled with the Spirit, they allowed Him to direct and empower
their life.

It is important to note that the extra oil had to be bought by the foolish virgins (v.9). While the indwelling spirit is a free gift from God that cannot be bought, being filled by the Holy Spirit involves effort on the part of the Christian, requiring our submission to Him (Galatians 5:16-25) in order to crucify the flesh and allow Him complete control. As a result, the 5 wise virgins were properly equipped when the Bridegroom arrived. The wise virgins were ready because of their faithfulness, while the foolish virgins were not prepared due to their own lethargy in providing their extra measure of oil to keep their lamps burning.

Are you a wise or foolish virgin today? If you are not sure, please consider making the following prayer right now:

> "Dear God in Heaven, I realize that I have not really been living my life for you. I humbly turn to you right now and ask you to forgive me. Dear Jesus, please rule and reign in my heart and life. Please help me to live for you for whatever time remains. I pray that I may be accounted worthy and that I may be able to stand before you when you return. In Jesus' name, I pray. Amen"

Our prayer is that many who read this book will pray this prayer and ask the Lord to help them be prepared for His return. We know for certain Jesus will return very soon and we need to be ready every single day as we eagerly await His coming for us.

THE WISE VIRGINS
"They That Were Ready Went In with Him to the Marriage and the Door Was Shut."

Epilogue

If we are witnessing the final days before the rapture we must alert all of our friends and loved ones before it is too late. We cannot allow the fear of what others think of us to keep us from helping to get people prepared.

When the *great tribulation* period begins, you do not want to be here! Also, you do not want to have any of your friends or loved ones miss the rapture that is about to take place. If you think things have been bad since 2020, you have no idea what is in store after the Antichrist appears on the scene. Please see the next page for an overview of the things predicted for those who are left behind.

If Sultan Suleiman's decree in 1537 began the Second Fulfillment of Daniel's Seventy-week prophecy then the final 7-years began in 2020. We know that Enoch's life served as a type-picture of the Firstfruit believer and since his rapture took place on the Feast of Pentecost (Enoch's birthday) it is a highly likely time for the Firstfruit rapture.[5]

While we can not be certain that the Feast of Pentecost is the correct time for the rapture, the wise and faithful believers will take Matthew Henry's advice: *"Therefore every day and every hour we must be ready, and not off our watch any day in the year, or any hour in the day."* (Matthew Henry, Volume 5, p. 372)[6]

Eye has not seen, nor ear heard
nor have entered into the heart of man
the things which God has prepared
for those who love Him.
(1 Corinthians 2:9)

Do you love Him?
Jesus said, "If anyone loves Me,
he will keep My Word." (John 14:23)

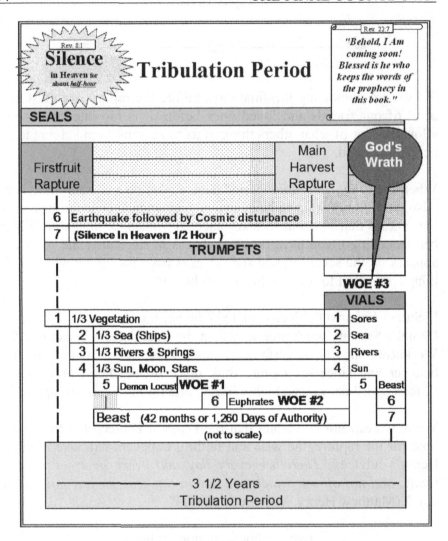

The above chart is an excerpt from Page 72 in our commentary on the book of Revelation entitled: *Calling All Overcomers*.

Supplemental Articles

Please see the Supplemental Articles on our website under the tab for our book entitled: *Daniel's Prophecies Unsealed* to find additional information on why there are only 3 ½ years remaining in the 70th week of Daniel between the Firstfruit Rapture and the end of the tribulation period. (www.ProphecyCountdown.com)

Reference Notes

As stated elsewhere in this book, we are indebted to Dr. Christian Widener for uncovering the final decree that everyone missed. He was kind enough to allow us to copy sections of his book: *Witnessing the End*. Since it has over 400 references, we are leaving his numbering intact for those wishing to study his valuable book more thoroughly.

Chapter 3 – Suleiman The Magnificent

1) Montefiore, Simon Sebag – *Jerusalem: The Biography,* Vintage Press © 2012, pp. 303-4.

2) Widener, Christian – *Witnessing The End*, End Times Berean © 2022, p. 156.

Chapter 4 – Timing of Christ's Second Coming

3) Ibid., pp. 157-160.

4) Ibid., pp. 163-164.

Epilogue

5) Mize, Lyn – *The Open Door*, Prophecy Countdown Publications, LLC © 2022. Please see Chapter 1 of his book for an excellent analysis of the Firstfruit rapture.

6) Since Suleiman restored Jerusalem between 1537-1541, it is possible that the start date for the decree may be off by a year or so. However, the best evidence points to 1537, because of other corroborating evidence Dr. Christian Widener gives in his book, particularly his case for the <u>Jubilee cycle ending in 2027</u>. In addition, Appendix 4 presents valuable evidence from Jared Kushner's book: *Breaking History* that the peace covenants made with many nations <u>crucially marked 2020</u> as the start of the final 70th Week in the Second Fulfillment of Daniel's Seventy Week prophecy.

Appendix 1 and 2 – Daniel's 70 Weeks

Footnotes from *Daniel's Prophecies Unsealed* can be found at the end of each appendix.

Appendix 3 – The Temple

Footnotes in this appendix can be found in *Witnessing the End*, by Dr. Christian Widener.

Appendix 5 – Signs of Christ's Coming

Footnotes for this appendix are located at the very end.

Appointed Time Is Here

2 Timothy 2:15 (KJ) admonishes us: *"Study to shew thyself approved unto God, a workman that needeth not be ashamed, rightly dividing the word of truth."* He goes on to say in 2 Timothy 3:16: *"All scripture is given by inspiration of God, and is profitable for doctrine, for reproof, for correction, for instruction in righteousness."*

Many Christians immediately scoff whenever someone discusses a possible time for Christ's return. This attitude breaks the Lord's heart, for He wants His Bride to be watching and He wants us all to remain teachable and humble under His Word.

The purpose of this book is to alert everyone as to the lateness of the hour…To the Bride of Christ to get her wedding garments made ready
(Revelation 19:7-9) and made spotless (Ephesians 5:27).
To the lost sinners of the world to turn to Jesus.

Habakkuk 2:3 (NIV) says, *"For the revelation awaits **an appointed time**; it speaks of the end and will not prove false. Though it linger, wait for it; **it will certainly come** and will not delay."*

The Lord has APPOINTED a time when He plans to bring an end to all things. Time is quickly running out, the APPOINTED time is here.

God wants us to be aware of the time He will return; His Second Coming is one of the central doctrines of His Word. He told us we should be WATCHING, and He gave many wonderful clues to those who will diligently study His Word. The words of the Prophet Daniel are very timely for the days we are living in:

9) "Go on your way, Daniel," he replied, "for the words are closed up and sealed ***until the time of the end***. 10) Many will be **purified**, made **spotless**, and **refined**, but the wicked will continue to act wickedly. None of the wicked will understand, but the wise will understand" (Daniel 12:9-10 – BSB).

And as the Apostle John so aptly put it: "Everyone who has this hope (of Christ's return) in him **purifies** himself, just as He is **pure**" (1 John 3:3). The message of Christ's soon return will purify the hearts of those who are His children. It is time for all of us to purify our hearts to be properly prepared when Jesus returns for us.

Bibliography

Commentaries on the Book of Daniel

Barnes, Albert – *Notes on the Bible: Daniel*, Baker Books © 1853 [Dan 9C] *

Carroll, B. H. – *An Interpretation of the English Bible: Daniel and the Inter-Biblical Period* (Available on Amazon or from: www.SolidChristianBooks.com) [Dan 9 C]**

Duguid, Ian M. – *Daniel*, P&R Publishers © 2008 [Dan 9C]

Emerson, Wallace L. – *Unlocking the Mysteries of Daniel*, Promise Publishing Co. © 1988 ***

Fausset, A.R. – *The Book of Daniel* (Available from the Blue Letter Bible (www.BlueLetterBible.org) [Dan 9C] *

Ferguson, Sinclair B. – *Daniel: The Preacher's Commentary*, Thomas Nelson Publishers © 1988 [Dan 9C] *

Hahn, Scott and Mitch, Curtis – *Daniel: The Ignatius Catholic Study Bible*, Ignatius Press © 1966 [Dan 9C] *

Henry, Matthew – *An Exposition: The Book of the Prophet Daniel*, Fleming H. Revell Co, Published in 1710 [Dan 9C]

Hewitt, Clarence H. – *The Seer of Babylon: Studies In The Book Of Daniel*, Kessinger Legacy Reprints, Advent Christian Publication Society © 1948 [Dan 9C] **

Jerome, St. – *Jerome's Commentary on Daniel* (translated by Gleason Archer), Wipf & Stock Publishers ©1958 [Dan 9C]

Miller, Stephen R. – *Daniel: The New American Commentary*, B&H Publishing Group © 1994 **

Mize, Lyn – *Daniel* © n/a (Available at: www.ffwfthb.org) **

Thomson, J.E.H. – *The Pulpit Commentary: Daniel*, W.M. Eerdmans Publishing Co. © 1981 [Dan 9C] **

Walvoord, John F. – *Daniel*, Moody Publishers © 2012

Young, Edward J. – *The Prophecy of Daniel*, W.M. Eerdmans Publishing Co. © 1949 [Dan 9C] **

[Dan 9C] Daniel 9 is rightly shown as Christ, not the Antichrist.

* Most useful commentaries in this author's opinion.

Other Books Quoted or Consulted

Anderson, Sir Robert – *The Coming Prince*, Kregel Publications © 1984 (Original 1894)

Coerper, Steve – *The "Daily [Sacrifice]" or "The Blameless"?*, Anakypto Forum Article, www.RogerShermanSociety.org

Deal, Colin – *The Great Tribulation: How Long?*, End Time News © 1991, P.O. Box 455, Rutherford College, NC 28671 [Dan 9C]

Hengstenberg, E.W. – *Christology of the Old Testament*, Forgotten Books © 2015 (Original 1864) [Dan 9C]

Jones, Dr. Floyd Nolen – *The Chronology of the Old Testament*, Master Books © 1993, New Leaf Press © 2005 [Also see the *Supplemental Articles* for *Daniel's Prophecies Unsealed*.]

Larkin, Rev. Clarence – *Second Coming of Christ*, Rev. Clarence Larkin Estate © 1918-1922. The picture shown in this book is used with permission of the Rev. Clarence Larkin Estate: P.O. Box 334, Glenside, PA 19038, USA, www.larkinestate.com

Mize, Lyn – *The Open Door*, Prophecy Countdown Publications, LLC © 2022, www.ProphecyCountdown.com

Mauro, Philip – *The Seventy Weeks and the Great Tribulation*, Master Books © 2015 [Dan 9C]

Montefiore, Simon Sebag – *Jerusalem: The Biography*, Vintage Press A Division of Random House © 2012

Panton, D. M. – *The Judgment Seat of Christ*, Schoettle Publishing Co. Inc., © 1984, www.schoettlepublishing.com

Simpson, Albert B. – *The Christ In The Bible Commentary: Volume Six*, Christian Publications © 1994

Widener, Christian – *Witnessing The End: Daniel's Seventy Sevens and the Final Decree Everyone Missed*, End Times Berean © 2022, www.WitnessingtheEnd.com

Widener, Christian – *The Temple Revealed*, End Times Berean © 2022, www.EndTimesBerean.com

Winter, Milo – *The Aesop for Children: with Pictures*, Rand McNally & Co., 1919 [in Public Domain] www.read.gov/aesop/043.html

[Dan 9C] Daniel 9 is rightly shown as Christ, not the Antichrist.

Appendix 1 – Daniel's 70 Weeks

Please read Daniel 9, prior to reading this appendix:	
	Verses
Daniel's Prayer for His People	1 to 19
Gabriel's Answer	20 to 27
Seventy Weeks Prophecy	24 to 27

The date for this chapter was around 537 BC and Daniel was studying the Scriptures relating to the seventy years of exile for his people and the desolation of the city of Jerusalem. According to Jeremiah 25:11; 29:4-10, he realized that their time of captivity was almost over (606 BC less 70 years = 536 BC). Daniel was a devout man of God who greatly mourned for what had befallen his people because of their rebellion against God. He earnestly poured out his heart asking for forgiveness and restoration.

> *And I prayed to the LORD my God, and made confession, and said, "O Lord, **great** and **awesome God**, who **keeps His covenant** and **mercy** with **those who love Him**, and with **those who keep His commandments**...'* (Daniel 9:4)

He realized they had been taken into Babylon because they had not really loved God nor kept His commandments. They had not repented of their evil ways after the Lord had sent prophets admonishing them. Their seventy years were about to expire, and Daniel was seeking the Lord for himself and his people.

He was told by the angel Gabriel *"thou art greatly beloved"* (Daniel 9:23). God greatly loved Daniel and He sent his holy messenger to answer his prayer the very moment he began to make his pleas.

> *23) At the **beginning** of your supplications the command went out, and **I have come to tell you**, for you are **greatly beloved**; therefore consider the matter, and **understand the vision**:*

> *24)* ***Seventy weeks*** *are determined for your people and for your holy city, to finish the transgression, to make an end of sins, to make reconciliation for iniquity, to bring in everlasting righteousness, to seal up vision and prophecy, and to anoint the Most Holy* (Daniel 9:23-24).

In answer to Daniel's prayer, the Lord revealed His plans: not only would He restore His people and His Holy city, but He also gave him a vision that would span over the next seventy weeks of years or 490 years. In other words, the Jews were driven into captivity for seventy years because of their sins, but now God was going to restore them over a period of 490 years (seventy weeks of years). This extended period of grace is a reflection of the unlimited forgiveness Jesus would bring. God's mercy was alluded to when Peter asked Jesus if he should forgive a brother seven times. Jesus said to him, "*I do not say to you, up to seven times, but up to **seventy times seven**"* (Mat 18:22).

The seventy weeks vision given to Daniel is a picture of God's ultimate plan to bring forgiveness to the entire world through a new covenant (see Jeremiah 31:31-34). From the time of the early church, this vision has always been applied to the Messiah, fulfilling the six purposes given (Hewitt, p. 253).

Doing Away With Sin[1]
finish the transgression – Israel's sins / Forgiveness of all sins
make an end of sins – Hebrews 10:1-18
make reconciliation for iniquity – Hebrews 9:26-28 One sacrifice

Bringing the Good News[2]
bring in everlasting righteousness – 2 Corinthians 5:21
seal up vision and prophecy – Luke 16:16
anoint the Most Holy – Anointing church at Pentecost (Acts 2)

The six distinct things listed were all fulfilled by the coming of the Messiah, who was God's final atonement for mankind. All of these purposes were accomplished during these seventy weeks of years. Gabriel then explains how this extended period of grace will be accomplished.

> The vision is broken down into the following segments:
>   v. 25   v. 26   v.27
> 7 weeks + 62 weeks + 1 week (½ + ½) = 70 weeks

25) Know therefore and understand, that from the going forth of the command to <u>restore and build Jerusalem</u> until Messiah the Prince, there shall be seven weeks and sixty-two weeks; the street shall be built again, and the wall, even in troublesome times (Daniel 9:25).

In order to understand the entire vision, we first need to determine the correct starting point. Based upon the above verse, we must find where *the command to restore and build Jerusalem* took place.   The following Scriptures should be considered:

Ezra 1:1-3 1st Year of Cyrus Proclamation to Build Temple	**Ezra 4:24; 6:7,8** 2nd Year of Darius Reaffirmation to Rebuild Temple
Ezra 7:8, 11-26 7th Year of Artaxerxes Authorize Ezra to Restore Temple	**Nehemiah 2:1-9** 20th Year of Artaxerxes Authorize to Finish <u>Rebuilding Jerusalem</u>

There is very little unanimity among expositors over which of the above four decrees is the correct starting point for Daniel's vision.[3] This is easily resolved when we see Nehemiah's prayer for the restoration of the city (Nehemiah 1). God quickly answered his prayer, and King Artaxerxes gave him authorization to rebuild it almost immediately. Daniel's divine vision refers to restoring and rebuilding the city, including the streets and walls during times of trouble. Notice how Nehemiah describes the situation:

Come and let us build the wall of Jerusalem, that we may no longer be a reproach..." "...half of my servants worked at construction, while the other half held the spears, the shields, the bows, and wore armor; and the leaders were behind all the house of Judah (Neh 2:17; 4:16).

Nehemiah's account of his mission plainly shows the *troublesome times* that the angel Gabriel must have referred to. We believe that it clearly aligns with the requirements given in Daniel's vision of the seventy weeks, which places the correct starting point of this key prophecy at the 20th year of King Artaxerxes' reign. As noted by one eminent commentator: "This is the first and only royal decree granting permission to "restore and build Jerusalem" (Walvoord, p. 276).

20th Year of Artaxerxes

The next major difficulty in ascertaining the point to begin our timeline is determining when the 20th year of Artaxerxes actually occurred. The most popular date given by most scholars is around 445 or 444 BC. This is the time used by Sir Robert Anderson in his famous work **The Coming Prince**, in which he calculated the date Christ was crucified. His book has recently come under attack due to his use of a 360-day prophetic year that one commentator noted was "a mode of reckoning, which was never adopted by the Hebrews, and therefore is so thoroughly destitute of foundation, that we need not stop to prove its incorrectness…" (Hengstenberg, p. 211).

Moreover, new evidence has recently been established that dates the 20th year of Artaxerxes as 454 BC.[4] Dr. Floyd Nolen Jones' significant work **The Chronology of the Old Testament** was first published in 1993. Dr. Jones's painstaking volume gives us a fresh new solution to Daniel's prophecy based upon a modification to the previous work of Ussher's monumental work **The Annals of the World**, published in 1658. With the biblically corrected date of 454 BC as the 20th year of King Artaxerxes, we have determined the proper starting point for Daniel's seventy weeks.

Interestingly, after we uncovered this correct beginning date, we found two older expositors who had previously determined Daniel's seventy weeks should also begin around 454 BC. Albert Barnes (1834)[5] arrived at 454 BC, while E. W. Hengstenberg (1864)[6] calculated 455 BC. These eminent scholars realized this important time well before recent expositors appeared creating unfounded interpretations based upon the erroneous date of 444–445 BC. Many of the traditions taught today were based upon this inaccurate chronology.

Timeline for Seventy Weeks

The timeline for the seventy weeks of years can be found at the end of this appendix on page 58. From the start date of 454 BC, the prophecy states we should move forward 7 weeks (49 years) and then another 62 weeks (434 years) for a total of 483 years. The remaining 1 week (7 years) follows the 483 years for a total of 490 years (7 x 70 weeks).

If we move forward from 454 BC by 49 years, we come to around 405 BC. While there are no known records in the Scripture that point to this exact moment in time, Albert Barnes noted: "the completion of the work undertaken by Nehemiah ...reached to the period here designated; and his last act as governor of Judea, in restoring the people and placing the affairs of the nation on its former basis, occurred at just about the period of the forty-nine years after the issuing of the command by Artaxerxes. That event, as is supposed above, occurred in 454 BC. The close of the seven weeks, or the forty-nine years, would therefore be 405 BC. This would be about the last year of the reign of Darius Nothus."[7]

...from the going forth of the command to restore and build Jerusalem until Messiah the Prince, there shall be <u>*seven weeks*</u> *and* <u>*sixty-two*</u> <u>*weeks*</u> (Daniel 9:25).

> The sixty-two weeks (434 years) takes us to 29-30 AD.
> (454 BC + 49 years + 434 years = 29-30 AD).

Christ's Ministry

The year 29-30 AD is the time when Jesus began His ministry as recorded in the four Gospels. He was baptized in the Jordan River and He preached about the coming Kingdom for a total of approximately 3½ years, after which He was crucified.

> *And after the sixty-two weeks Messiah shall be cut off, but not for Himself...* (Daniel 9:26)

Jesus was killed or *cut off* because the Jews rejected their Messiah and the Romans crucified Him on a cross, precisely as the Prophet Daniel saw in the vision the angel Gabriel had explained over twenty-five hundred years ago.

And he shall confirm (strengthen)[1396] the covenant with many for one week; and in the midst of the week He shall cause the sacrifice and the oblation to cease... (Daniel 9:27 – KJ)

Jesus began his ministry that was stopped halfway through (i.e., middle of seven years = 3½ years). Jesus had come to **strengthen** the covenant of love and mercy as mentioned previously in His prayer: *"O Lord, great and awesome God, who keeps His covenant and mercy..."* (Daniel 9:4)

The covenant that Daniel is referring to is the covenant of love and mercy that God made with his people. Notice what Jesus had to say regarding this covenant at the Last Supper:

> *And he said unto them, this is my blood of the new covenant which is shed for many* (Mark 14:24).

At the Last Supper, the Lord was revealing how the wine the disciples were about to drink represented the blood of a *new covenant*, which was about to be shed the very next day. His blood actually strengthens the original covenant because there would no longer be any need to continue to offer sacrifices to God (i.e., *He shall cause the sacrifice and the oblation to cease*). His act of love by dying on the cross ended sacrifices and made the original covenant a more durable covenant that would permanently bind His love to all of humanity.

The precious lifeblood of Jesus Christ is like superglue that forever binds God's covenant of love and mercy to mankind. His atonement creates an everlasting bond of God's love that can never be broken (*cf.* Hebrews 7:22-28; Hebrews 9:11-15).

Calling Cornelius After 3½ Years
Jesus was crucified in the middle of the seventieth week of Daniel (*in the midst of the week*) after which the Good News of the coming kingdom was preached to the people of Israel. Remember, the extended period of grace promised in Daniel's vision was for seventy weeks of years, i.e., 490 years. After Christ's death there still remained three and one-half years in order to fulfill God's purposes to

Jewish people.   Over this period the Gospel was preached almost exclusively to the Jews.

The confirmation of the new covenant to the people of Israel continued from the day of Pentecost when 3,000 Jews were saved, and as noted by another eminent commentator: "In that three and one-half years it is stated more than once that great numbers of Jews…were converted…one might safely conclude 100,000 Jews were converted and brought to the knowledge of the truth…" (Carroll, p. 133).

But Israel's extended day of grace came to an end when the Jews persecuted the Church and Stephen was stoned   (Acts 7:54-60).[8] Shortly thereafter, God's program turned from the Jewish people when the Apostle Peter received a supernatural vision. He was sent to the house of Cornelius, where he preached the Word of God and the Holy Spirit fell on the Gentiles for the first time.   Peter then commanded them to be baptized in the name of the Lord (please see Acts 10)[9].

Jesus alluded to this same time of 3½ years in His parable of the barren fig tree: *"…Look, for **three years** I have come seeking fruit on this **fig tree** and find none…But he said…let it alone this year also…and if it bears fruit well. But if not, **after that you can cut it down"** (Luke 13:7-8).

Destruction of Jerusalem
Once the people of Israel failed to bear fruit, the final week ended. The seventy weeks (490 years) in Daniel's vision were completed, and God turned his attention to the Gentiles with the conversion of Cornelius. Since Israel rejected Christ and the Apostles' message, Jesus says the *fig tree* should be cut down.

Notice that the destruction of Jerusalem and the Temple occurs after the seventy weeks are completed. The prince who was to come was Titus who led the Roman armies. Jesus also alluded to this time: *"But when you see Jerusalem surrounded by armies, then know that its desolation is near"* (Luke 21:20).

...and the people of the prince who is to come shall destroy the city and the sanctuary. The end of it shall be with a flood, and till the end of the war desolations are determined (Daniel 9:26).

Abomination of Desolation

The Jewish people had been given an extended period of grace of seventy weeks or 490 years. They crucified the Messiah and rejected the message the Apostles brought to save them. To make matters even worse, they continued to offer sacrifices in their Temple, which truly was an abomination in God the Father's eyes after they had rejected the sacrifice of His Son.

As noted by Hengstenberg, "The ancient temple is...changed, on account of the unbelief of the [Jewish] people and the murder of the Messiah, from a house of God into a house of abomination, which must be destroyed" (Hengstenberg, p. 169).

Because of this, God had the Roman armies sweep into Jerusalem to desolate the city and the Temple: *"...and for the overspreading of abominations he shall make it desolate, even until the consummation, and that determined shall be poured upon the desolate"* (Daniel 9:27– KJ).

This shows that the flood of God's wrath against the Jews was because they continued to offer sacrifices in the Temple, which was the abomination that forced Him to send Titus to desolate the city. This desolation will continue until the consummation when the times of the Gentiles are completed.[10]

The vision of the seventy weeks is a magnificent prophecy of God sending His Son to redeem all of mankind. Even though Israel rejected their Messiah, God is not finished with them.

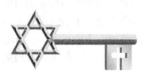

"A remnant of them will return; the <u>destruction decreed</u> shall <u>overflow with righteousness</u>. For the Lord God of hosts will make a determined end in the midst of the land" (Isaiah 10:22-23).

*"...that **blindness in part has happened to Israel** until **the fullness of the Gentiles** has come in. And so **all Israel will be saved**... "* (Romans 11:25-26).

In 1948, we witnessed the beginning of the return of the remnant. The story is not quite over, but the time of the end is rapidly approaching.

The chart on the following page is the one that was included in our book: *Daniel's Prophecies Unsealed*, which was published in 2018. It is based upon using the decree found in Nehemiah 2:1-9 as outlined above.

The chart that can be found on the facing page has been adjusted to use the decree that Dr. Christian Widener utilized in his book: *Witnessing The End* (based upon Ezra 7:8, 11-26). We have adjusted the chart he has on page 150, of his book to show a slightly different interpretation of the final 70th week. Instead of using his 7-year period for Christ's ministry, we show this 7-year period as divided into two parts: (1) the traditional 3 ½ years of ministry followed by (2) the 3 ½ year period following the crucifixion. During this time the Gospel was preached almost exclusively to the Jews until the Apostle Peter was sent to the house of Cornelius. There he preached the Word of God and the Holy Spirit fell on the Gentiles for the first time.

Summary
In *Daniel's Prophecies Unsealed* we used 3 BC for the birth of Christ and a ministry start date of 29/30 AD with the Seventy Weeks ending in 36/37 AD. Dr. Christian Widener makes a good case for a start date of 27 AD, which appears to line up with his computation for the Jubilee years. Under this scenario, the Seventy Weeks would end in 33/34 AD.
While we cannot be dogmatic as to which model is correct, we believe either one shows that the Seventy Weeks (490 Years) were fulfilled at Christ's first coming.

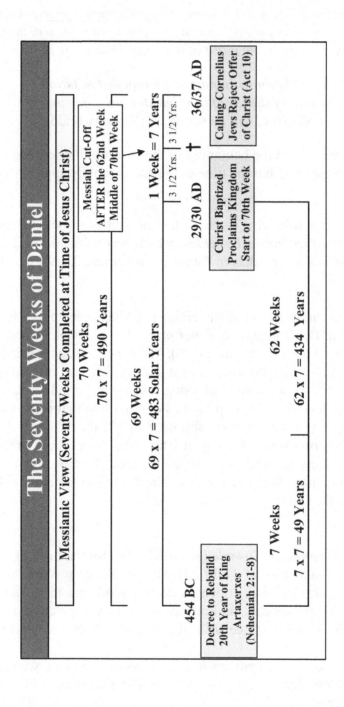

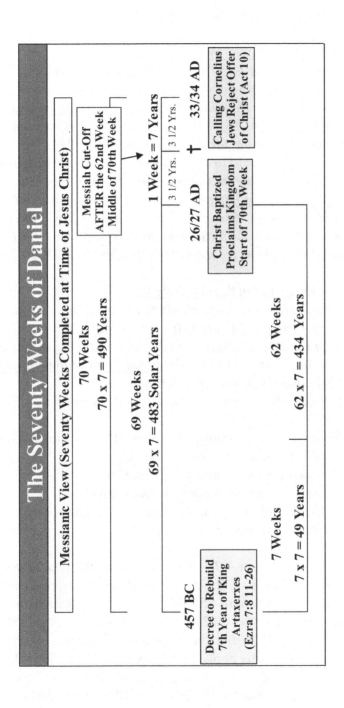

Footnotes – Appendix 1

1) Scriptures for <u>Doing Away With Sin</u>:
"16) 'This is the covenant that I will make with them after those days, says the Lord: I will put My laws into their hearts, and in their minds I will write them,' 17) then He adds, '<u>Their sins and their lawless deeds I will remember no more.</u>' 18 Now where there is remission of these, there is no longer an offering for sin" (Hebrews 10:16-18).
"26) He then would have had to suffer often since the foundation of the world; but now, once at the end of the ages, He has appeared <u>to put away sin by the sacrifice of Himself.</u> 27) And as it is appointed for men to die once, but after this the judgment, 28) so Christ was offered once to bear the sins of many. To those who eagerly wait for Him He will appear a second time, apart from sin, for salvation" (Heb 9:26-28).

2) Scriptures for <u>Bringing the Good News</u>:
"21) For He made Him who knew no sin to be sin for us, that we might become the <u>righteousness of God in Him</u>" (2 Cr 5:21).
"16) Until John the Baptist, the law of Moses and the messages of the prophets were your guides. But now the <u>Good News</u> of <u>the Kingdom of God is preached</u>, and everyone* is eager to get in"
(Luke 16:16 – NLT). *Or *"everyone is urged to enter in."*

3) The following is a sampling of a few of the various scholars' views on the starting point for Daniel's vision.

Ezr 1:1-3	Young, Keil, Mauro, Leupold, Calvin
Ezr 7:8	Archer, Hewitt, Miller, Wood, Carroll
Neh 2:1-8	Walvoord, Sir Robert Anderson, Hengstenberg, Barnes, Hoehner

4) Jones, Dr. Floyd Nolen – ***The Chronology of the Old Testament***, New Leaf Press © 2005, p. 237. While Dr. Jones does a masterful job in providing the correct date of 454 BC as the 20th year of Artaxerxes, he incorrectly assumes the 483-year period that ends in 30 AD represents the time that Christ died, instead of the time Christ was baptized, as outlined in this book. [Author's note: Using Dr. Christian Widener's 27 AD for the start of Christ's ministry could mean Dr. Nolen may have been correct with Christ's death being in 30 AD.]

Footnotes – Appendix 1 (Continued)

5) Barnes, Albert – *Notes on the Bible: Daniel,* Baker Books © 1853, pp. 165, 174.

6) Hengstenberg, E. W. – *Christology of the Old Testament,* Forgotten Books © 2015, originally published in 1864, p. 216.

7) Barnes, op. cit., p. 175. Barnes went on to say, "Nehemiah is known to have lived to a great age (Josephus)....he was thirty years old when first appointed governor of Judea, and that the time referred to at the close of the "seven weeks" (49 years), was the completion of his work in the restoration of the affairs of Jerusalem, the whole period would only reach to the seventy-ninth year of his age....What he did is recorded in Nehemiah 13:7-31. These included restoring the Sabbath to its proper observance which had become greatly disregarded...constraining unlawful marriages...put the affairs of the temple on their former basis...This was the termination of (their) captivity in the fullest sense...or constituted a 'period or epoch' in the history of the Jewish people." God used Nehemiah to restore both the city and the Temple in Jerusalem during the first part of his life. For the remainder of his life, he helped to restore people's spiritual lives.

[Readers are encouraged to read the entire book of Nehemiah in order to appreciate how the Lord used this faithful man of God to accomplish the first segment of Daniel's vital prophecy.]

8) Hewitt, Clarence H. – *The Seer of Babylon: Studies in the Book of Daniel,* Kessinger Legacy Reprints © 1948, p. 263: "...it is not difficult to believe that, had we the exact dates, we should find just seven years between Christ's baptism and the time when Israel definitely rejected the message of forgiveness by persecuting and scattering the disciples..." Hewitt also noted: "The last half week is an integral part of the whole. The seventy weeks measures Israel's added day of grace, and that day did not end with the Cross."

Footnotes – Appendix 1 (Continued)

9)   Thompson, J.E.H. – *The Pulpit Commentary: Daniel*, W.M. Eerdmans Publishing © 1981, p. 274. A similar view of this time was noted: "the covenant shall prevail for many during one week." This agrees with the first version we find in the Septuagint, The covenant– God's covenant with Israel...prevails with many; "his covenant to send a Messiah...would prevail with the hearts of many of Israel during one week. If we reckon our Lord's ministry to have begun in the year AD 30 and the conversion of St. Paul AD 37, we have the interval required."

10) Hewitt, op. cit., pp. 272-3, "The conclusion seems inescapable that...'the prince that shall come' shall make it 'desolate,' not for a time only but even 'unto the consummation of the present age,' Gabriel foretold this final desecration of that holy place at the hands of Titus...Such a conclusion of this remarkable vision is both suitable and significant...For the logical termination of the prophecy is the destruction of the city and its sanctuary, just as its beginning was the promulgation of an edict for their restoration."

Appendix 2 – The Abominations of Desolations

There are several cases where the Abominations of Desolations are mentioned in the book of Daniel, which has led to misinterpretation when not understood within the correct context. Here are four occurrences found in the book of Daniel:

False Prophet	Daniel 8:11-14
Destruction of Jerusalem	Daniel 9:27
Antiochus Epiphanes	Daniel 11:31
Antichrist	Daniel 12:11

In addition to the book of Daniel, the term is also found in the New Testament in several places. Jesus used the term in Luke 21:20, in predicting the destruction of Jerusalem when Titus surrounded Jerusalem in 70 AD, and it could also have its *second fulfillment* at the future battle of Armageddon when all of the nations come against Israel:

And they gathered them together to the place in Hebrew, Armageddon (Revelation 16:16).

16 And He has a name written on His robe and on His thigh:
    KING OF KINGS AND LORD OF LORDS.
17 Then I saw an angel standing in the sun, and he cried out in a loud voice to all the birds flying overhead, "Come, gather together for the great supper of God, 18 so that you may eat the flesh of kings and commanders and mighty men, of horses and riders, of everyone slave and free, small and great." 19 Then I saw the beast and the kings of the earth with their armies assembled to wage war against the One seated on the horse, and against His army. 20 But the beast was captured along with the false prophet, who on its behalf had performed signs deceiving those who had the mark of the beast and worshiped its image. Both the beast and the false prophet were thrown alive into the fiery lake of burning sulfur. 21 And the rest were killed with the sword that proceeded from the mouth of the one seated on the horse. (Revelation 19:16-21 – BSB)

Abominations of Desolations

Several cases of *"abomination of desolation"* are mentioned in Daniel.

Occurrence	Daniel
False Prophet	8:11-14
Destruction of Jerusalem	9:27
Antiochus Epiphanes	11:31
Antichrist	12:11

False Prophet (End of Great Tribulation)

*11) Yea, **he magnified himself** even to the **prince of the host**, and by him the daily [sacrifice] was taken away, and the place of his sanctuary was cast down. 12) And an host was given him against the daily [sacrifice] by reason of transgression, and it **cast down the truth** to the **ground**; and it practiced, and prospered. 13) Then I heard a holy one speaking,..... 'For how long is the vision concerning... the* <u>transgression that makes desolate</u>, *and the giving over of the sanctuary and* <u>host to be trampled underfoot?</u>' *14) And he said to me, for 2,300 evenings and mornings [1,150 days]*[1] *Then the **sanctuary shall be restored to its rightful state"** (Daniel 8:13-14– ESV). In chapter 3 of **Daniel's Prophecies Unsealed** we learned that the *little horn* of Daniel 8 represents the *false prophet* who will **cast down truth to the ground** (deceive many) at the time of the end (p. 38-40). The *false prophet* will persecute the saints (<u>*host to be trampled underfoot*</u>), causing the <u>*transgression that makes desolate*</u>, after which time they will be restored in the New Jerusalem (Revelation 21:2, 9-10). This period of 1,150 days will end toward the very end of the tribulation period.

Destruction of Jerusalem (70 AD)

As we learned in Appendix 1, the <u>*abomination of desolation*</u> in Daniel 9:27 was the fact that the Jewish people <u>continued to offer sacrifices</u> in the Temple even after Jesus had made the ultimate sacrifice of dying for all of humanity. Because of this, the city of Jerusalem was destroyed by Titus in 70 AD just as Jesus had predicted: *"But when you see Jerusalem surrounded by armies, then know that its desolation is near"* (Luke 21:20) [+ 2nd fulfillment at end of Tribulation].[2]

Antiochus Epiphanes (165 BC)

The *abomination of desolation* in Daniel 11:31 was created by Antiochus Epiphanes when he set up a statue of Jupiter in the Temple and sacrificed a hog on the altar. This abomination took place in 165 BC and was not the desolations Jesus referred to in Matthew 24 or Luke 21.

Antichrist (Beginning of Great Tribulation)

Jesus made another prediction about a future *abomination of desolation*, which He said Daniel referred to:

> *15) Therefore when you see the* *abomination of desolation,* *spoken of by Daniel the prophet,* *standing in the holy place* *(whoever reads, let him understand)...21) For then there will be* *great tribulation, such as has not been since the beginning of the world until this time, no, nor ever shall be.*
> (Matthew 24:15, 21)
> *And from the time that the daily [sacrifice] is taken away, and the* *abomination of desolation* *is set up, there shall be one thousand two hundred and ninety days [1,290 days]*
> (Daniel 12:11).

The *abomination* that Jesus referred to in Matthew concerns the time of *great tribulation* during the final 3½ years before the second coming. The Apostle Paul described the leader (Antichrist) during this period as follows:

> *(3) that **man of sin** be revealed, the son of perdition; (4) Who opposeth and **exalteth himself** above all that is called God, or that is worshipped; so that he as God **sitteth in the temple of God,** shewing himself that **he is God*** (2 Thessalonians 2:3-4).

The Antichrist will cause another *abomination of desolation* when he arrives in Jerusalem claiming to be God at the start of the great tribulation.

Footnotes – Appendix 2

1) (Miller, Stephen R. p. 228): "Most scholars believe that 2,300 evenings and mornings involve only a total of 1,150 days, since the 1,150 evening and 1,150 morning sacrifices...equal a total of 2,300."

2) The 2nd fulfillment that is described on the previous page (p.63).

How Long is a Generation?

*Now learn a parable of the fig tree; When his branch is yet tender, and putteth forth leaves, ye know that summer is nigh: So likewise ye, when ye shall see all these things, know that it is near, even at the doors. Verily I say unto you, **This generation shall not pass, till all these things be fulfilled**.* (Matthew 24:32-34 – KJV)

What was the average life expectancy at the time of Jesus?

Those living in the days of **Jesus** (as mentioned in the New Testament) had an **average life span** that was similar to human life spans before the arrival of modern medicine and technology. At the time Jesus spoke the above words, the **average life expectancy** was around 30 to 35 years, similar to the **life span** of those in classical Rome.

> 32 AD + 35 = 67 AD around the time that the Romans' siege of Jerusalem began (3½ years of judgment), ending in 70 AD.

In 1948 the average life expectancy was approximately 70 years (or 80 because of strength, as in Psalm 90).

> 1948 + 70 = 2018 +?

*The days of our life are **seventy years**— Or even, if because of strength, **eighty years**; Yet their pride [in additional years] is only labor and sorrow, For it is soon gone and we fly away.* (Psalm 90:10 – AMP)

Appendix 3 – The Temple Mount

One big question people have regarding the timing of end-time events is how can the Antichrist proclaim himself to be God in the temple when the temple has not been built? A related question is how he can confirm a peace treaty that has already been signed. The purpose of this appendix is to address these types of questions and provide some plausible explanations.

Remember in chapter 3, we discussed the dual application to Scripture and how Daniel's 70 Weeks applied to Jesus fulfilling the first application with His First Coming and how the second application will be tied to the Antichrist in Christ's Second Coming.

> He will confirm a covenant with many
> for one 'seven.' In the middle of the 'seven'
> he will put an end to sacrifice and offering.
> And *at the temple* he will set up an abomination
> that causes desolation, until the end
> that is decreed is poured out on him.
> (Daniel 9:27 – NIV)

First, let's look at the first part of this verse. Notice that the Antichrist only confirms the covenant with many other nations. It does not say that he drew up the treaty, but he merely confirms it. Dr. Christian Widener's observations are quite perceptive:

> "The mention of confirming the covenant does not necessarily mean that the Antichrist is the one who drafts the treaty or declaration. He just must somehow lend his support to it. The statement, *"with the many"* is likely an allusion to the many nations that will likewise support it in a collective peace deal or agreement. In the process, they will acknowledge Israel's right to exist as a nation—and that their right to the land comes from God, through the Abrahamic Covenant. Also, the Antichrist will just be one of the participants in the whole affair.

And it may not be obvious that he soon will be the Beast that begins to rule the nations of the earth three and a half years later in the great tribulation. Furthermore, since there will only be seven years left for human government until the return of Christ, this means that any *"confirmation of the covenant"* will be *de facto* for seven years, so the treaty doesn't have to specify seven years in its terms." (Widener, p.303)

Remember that President Trump sponsored the *"Peace to Prosperity"* plan in January 2020, which was almost exactly 483 years from the time Sultan Suleiman issued his decree to rebuild areas on the Temple Mount in 1537. This 181-page document can be downloaded on our website under the **Supplemental Articles** for our book: **Daniel's Prophecies Unsealed** www.ProphecyCountdown.com

"Then later that same year, the Abraham Accords emerged and presented **a viable candidate for the fulfillment of Daniel's prophecy**. Many wondered whether the accords would survive the transition to a new democratic administration in the U.S. under President Biden; however, when the Abraham Accords passed their one-year anniversary, not only were they still in place, but they were also bearing fruit! The accords were then embraced by the Biden administration and have continued to flourish. Indeed, it was soon evident that they were not just another peace deal fiasco, but instead were potentially something prophetically significant.
Then came the Abraham Accords,[298] which included official recognition of the State of Israel by the Arab countries who signed it, and it began opening **a new era of peace in the region**.[299] Securing peace with Israel's neighbors is a big step toward securing peace with the Palestinians since their cause has usually been universally supported by the Muslim nations. The more they lose that support, though, the more pressure they have to actually negotiate a resolution to the conflict." (Widener, pp 304-5) [Emphasis added]

Readers can read and download all of these historic peace agreements that are located beneath the *"Peace to Prosperity"* plan mentioned above.

It appears that President Donald Trump may have initiated the final peace initiative alluded to by the Prophet Daniel right before our eyes. The covenants were signed by the leaders in Israel along with the nations from the Kingdom of Bahrain, the Kingdom of Morocco, the Republic of Sudan, and the United Arab Emirates.

It may be noteworthy that several of these Abrahamic Accords were also signed by former Prime Minister Benjamin Netanyahu. As of this writing, the current government in Israel has been dissolved with Benjamin Netanyahu being reelected as the Prime Minister who has said that he wants to form a wide national government. This has set the stage for the return to power by Israel's longtime leader who helped initiate the Abraham Accords in 2020. He will now be in place when the Antichrist appears on the scene very shortly. When the Antichrist does appear he could *confirm the covenant with many* (Daniel 9:27) simply by signing onto the Accords that have already been put in place and previously signed by the *many* nations.

Remember, the covenant does not need to be a 7-year agreement. It is a 7-year covenant by virtue of the fact that it only has a period of 7 years before the 70th Week is completed. I think that we have all been guilty of reading something into the prophecy that is not there.

Reinstating Sacrifices on the Temple Mount

> In the middle of the 'seven'
> he will put an end to sacrifice and offering.
> And *at the temple* he will set up an abomination
> that causes desolation, until the end
> that is decreed is poured out on him.
> (Daniel 9:27 – NIV)

We will now address the issue of how the Antichrist will put an end to the sacrifices that haven't even started yet. It says that he will bring them to an end 'in the middle" of the seven-year period. If the final 70th Week of Daniel began sometime in 2020, then we are approaching the halfway mark someplace between the middle of 2023 or the middle of 2024.

This would mean that animal sacrifices would need to begin sometime in 2023 or the following year (2024) at the latest.

> "Then after the Abraham Accords were inaugurated in 2020, people started asking the question of whether it was time to normalize the Temple Mount, meaning to allow equal access to the site that is held to be holy by Muslims, Jews, and Christians.[302] This would mean recognizing that all faiths should be allowed to have access to and pray on the Temple Mount, as well as allowing them to celebrate their respective religious festivals and observances. This is **exactly what was called for in** the *Peace to Prosperity* plan that was approved by both the U.S. and Israel.[303] Soon after, Jews began to be allowed to pray openly and to be given access through gates that normally were only open to Muslims.[304] This was followed up by the first legal decision of the courts declaring that it was not illegal for Jews to pray on the Temple Mount.[305] While not explicit in Scripture, one of the necessary preconditions for restoring sacrifices is the ability to pray openly on the Temple Mount....but with all the preparations that have been made, **there is good reason to believe that this prophecy will soon be fulfilled literally**. It may not be a return to full sacrificial services, with the slaughter of thousands of animals, **but some form of priestly sacrifice could once again be seen in Israel.**"
> [Emphasis added] (Widener, pp. 307-8)

But doesn't the Temple need to be rebuilt in order to have animal sacrifices? Not necessarily. In an article that can be downloaded from our website, the Sanhedrin are citing Donald Trump's Israel-Palestine peace plan and claim that it gives them the authority and approval to begin reinstating sacrifices on the Temple Mount. It's entitled: ***Thanks to Trump: Pascal Lamb Could Be Sacrificed on Temple Mount for the First Time in 2,000 Years***. This fascinating article is located under the ***Supplemental Articles*** for our book: ***Daniel's Prophecies Unsealed***.

The Sanhedrin has constructed a temporary altar that can be transported to the Temple Mount and then removed once the ceremony has been completed. Rabbi Weiss, the Sanhedrin spokesman has said:

"The only thing preventing the Jewish people from performing the Passover Sacrifices is the Israeli government."

The sacrifices mentioned in Daniel 9:27 do not require an actual rebuilt Temple. The sacrifices only require an altar that is built to adhere to Biblical requirements. The Sanhedrin has already constructed such a structure that is ready to be put into use! With Benjamin Netanyahu being reelected, perhaps his new government will be friendly towards the Sanhedrin and allow them to perform the sacrifice at the Temple Mount on their temporary altar.

Abomination of Desolation
In Appendix 2, we listed the four cases where the term: Abomination of Desolation is used in the book of Daniel. The last case mentioned has to do with the Antichrist appearing on the Temple Mount at the beginning of the *great tribulation.*

> *5) Therefore when you see the abomination of desolation, spoken of by Daniel the prophet, standing in the holy place (whoever reads, let him understand)...21) For then there will be great tribulation, such as has not been since the beginning of the world until this time, no, nor ever shall be.*
> (Matthew 24:15, 21)

This warning was given by our Lord just before His crucifixion. He was warning the Church of the Antichrist who the Apostle Paul also warned us about in 2 Thessalonians 2:3-4.

Notice that Jesus tells us that he will be standing in the holy place. Some have taken this to mean that he is standing in the Temple, but Dr. Christian Widener's take may be more accurate:

"We might consider, however, that the references to the Antichrist standing in the "temple" and causing the abomination of desolation, mentioned in Matthew 24 and 2 Thessalonians 2, might simply refer to **the Temple Mount area** and not a rebuilt structure. In the book of Acts, we read that the disciples were meeting daily in the temple (*hieron* - Strong's G2411).

This word applies broadly to mean a temple and its entire designated area, so it is often translated "temple courts" because the context makes it clear that they were not in the temple building itself, but in the Temple Mount complex, or the courts of the temple.

When we read the passages in Acts 2:46 and 5:25 that describe believers in the temple (*hieron*) it is understood that the whole area, including the courts and the temple building, was included. However, when Paul wrote in 2 Thessalonians 2:4 that the man of lawlessness would set *"himself up in God's temple, proclaiming himself to be God,"* he used a different word, ***naos*** (Strong's G3485), which specifically refers to the innermost holy place of a temple building itself.

However, the Dome of the Spirits stands over the area that was once the threshing floor of Araunah, where the ***holy of holies*** of the **temple** once sat.[317] If the Antichrist made his declaration of being God while standing at or near this spot on the Temple Mount, then I would say that this could also satisfy the grammatical usage of the word ***naos***, **without a building**."[Emphasis added]
(Widener, pp. 313-15)

In Dr. Christian Widener's first book: *The Temple Revealed*, he discovered the true location of the Temple. His painstaking research showed that the holy of holies of the Temple once stood where the Dome of the Spirits is located as shown in the photographs on the facing page, as well as the back cover of this book.

This area is north of the Dome of the Rock and it is the area where a future Temple could be rebuilt without disturbing that area. More likely, it may be the location where the Antichrist will come to hold a press conference to publicly declare that he is taking over control of the world because he is god (Daniel 9:27 and 2 Thessalonians 2:4).

Jesus Laments Over Jerusalem

37 O Jerusalem, Jerusalem, who kills the prophets and stones those sent to her, how often I have longed to gather your children together, as a hen gathers her chicks under her wings, but you were unwilling! 38 Look, *your house* is left to you desolate. 39 For I tell you that you will not see Me again until you say, 'Blessed is He who comes in the name of the Lord. *e*' *e* 39 Psalm 118:26 (Matthew 23:37-39 – BSB)

Just before Jesus was about to be crucified He lamented over Jerusalem. The religious leaders had turned the Temple from a house of God to "*your house*" because the Jews had made it a den of robbers (Matthew 21:13). Because of this, Jesus said it would be desolate, which was fulfilled when Titus destroyed the city in 70 AD.

Much of the drama in *The Final Countdown* has centered around one of the most valued pieces of real estate in the world. The Temple Mount will become center stage once again as events during these closing years come to their final conclusion.

After the desolation of Jerusalem in 70 AD, Sultan Suleiman was given a dream that he was to rebuild the walls of Jerusalem and beautify the Temple Mount. Suleiman the Magnificent was God's chosen vessel to fulfill Isaiah's prophecy of rebuilding God's Holy City of Jerusalem. In 1537 he issued his decree that was placed on the Temple Mount (preserved in stone) for future generations to see.

The **Peace to Prosperity** plan was issued in January 2020 along with the **Abraham Accords** in September 2020. These covenants occurred 483 years (69 Weeks x 7) after Suleiman's decree in 1537. The final Seven Years may have begun in 2020, which will culminate with Jesus Christ returning in 2027. In this Second Fulfillment of the Seventy Weeks of Daniel, the world will witness the Antichrist making his appearance on the Temple Mount. This will begin the final 3 ½ years of Great Tribulation:

> 5) Therefore when you see the <u>abomination of desolation</u>, spoken of by Daniel the prophet, <u>standing in the holy place</u> (whoever reads, let him understand)...21) For then there will be <u>great tribulation</u>, such as has not been since the beginning of the world until this time, no, nor ever shall be.
> (Matthew 24:15, 21)

The good news is that Jesus will be coming back at the end of this time to restore this fallen world. Now is the time to prepare ourselves and help others prepare. As Jesus warns in the above verse, the time of the **great tribulation** will be unlike any other time since the world began. We don't want to be here when that time arrives. Jesus does provide a way of escape for those **blameless** believers (2 Peter 3:14) who are ready when the time arrives.

Jesus told us that we should be praying to be accounted worthy to escape the time that is coming.

> 34) And take heed to yourselves, lest at anytime your hearts be overcharged with surfeiting, and drunkenness, and cares of this life, and so that day come upon you unawares. 35) For as a snare shall it come on all them that dwell on the face of the whole earth. 36) **Watch ye therefore, and <u>pray always</u>, that ye may be <u>accounted worthy</u> to <u>escape</u> all these things that shall come to pass, and to stand before the Son of man.** (Luke 21:34-36 – KJV)

The faithful, overcomer heeds the Lord's advice and continually **prays for deliverance** from the coming Tribulation period.

Food for Thought – Possible Interpretation of Daniel 12:11

Daniel's final vision ends by giving several counts of days that have remained a mystery, which are shrouded by possible mistranslations. Perhaps *the daily* in Daniel 12:11 should have been translated: *the blameless[6],* and could be paraphrased:

> *And from the time that the* <u>*blameless are removed*</u>, *and the* <u>*abomination of desolation*</u> *is set up, there will be 1,290 days.*

This may be telling us that the blameless believers are removed to a place of safety away from the horrors of the Great Tribulation that is about to ensnare the world. Soon after the righteous are taken away, the Antichrist will arrive in Jerusalem claiming to be God (*cf.* Mat 24:15; 2Th 2:3-4, 7-8). The overcoming Christians are raptured and the Jewish remnant is taken to their place of safety in the wilderness.

The count of days Daniel recorded is probably meant to provide those living during that time a way of determining how much longer they will need to endure before Jesus Christ returns at His Second Coming.

6) *"<u>The daily</u>"* could be a cryptic reference to the **blameless believers**, whose lives are seen by God as daily sacrifices (per Romans 12:1), and that the *"taking away"* is the rapture of Firstfruit believers (*cf.* Rev 14:1-5). A friend of our ministry recently noted: "What if '<u>the-daily</u>', HaTamid (H8548), was incorrectly translated from Aramaic or a scribal error changed the Mem to a Dalet and should have been a noun version of HaTamim, from the same root word, meaning **the-blameless** (H8549) (as a noun, rendered 22 times in NAS)?" This verse could then be paraphrased:

> *"And from the time that the* <u>*blameless are removed*</u>, *and the* <u>*abomination of desolation*</u> *is set up, there will be 1,290 days."*

A reasonable inference from Daniel 12:11 might be that *"the blameless"* are taken away and the abomination of desolation is set up at the same time. This may suggest the removal of the *blameless* believers and then the Antichrist is revealed as Paul told us: *"He who now restrains will do so until* <u>*he is taken out of the way*</u>. *And* <u>*then the lawless one will be revealed*</u>"(2Th 2:7-8). See pp.102-107 in *Calling All Overcomers* for more information on the removal of the restrainer.

[The above is an excerpt from *Daniel's Prophecies Unsealed*]

The Shepherd Boy and the Wolf – An Æsop Fable

A Shepherd Boy tended his master's Sheep near a dark forest not far from the village. Soon he found life in the pasture very dull. All he could do to amuse himself was to talk to his dog or play on his shepherd's pipe.

One day as he sat watching the Sheep and the quiet forest, and thinking what he would do should he see a Wolf, he thought of a plan to amuse himself.

His Master had told him to call for help should a Wolf attack the flock, and the Villagers would drive it away. So now, though he had not seen anything that even looked like a Wolf, he ran toward the village shouting at the top of his voice, "Wolf! Wolf!"

As he expected, the Villagers who heard the cry dropped their work and ran in great excitement to the pasture. But when they got there they found the Boy doubled up with laughter at the trick he had played on them. A few days later the Shepherd Boy again shouted, "Wolf! Wolf!" Again the Villagers ran to help him, only to be laughed at again.

Then one evening as the sun was setting behind the forest and the shadows were creeping out over the pasture, a Wolf really did spring from the underbrush and fall upon the Sheep.

In terror, the Boy ran toward the village shouting "Wolf! Wolf!" But though the Villagers heard the cry, they did not run to help him as they had before. "He cannot fool us again," they said.

The Wolf killed a great many of the Boy's sheep and then slipped away into the forest.

So many dates have been set for the Lord's return that most people scoff whenever a new prognostication is made. As in the fable of the boy who cried, "Wolf," the real danger lies when the correct prediction is ignored and it actually proves to be true. The purpose of *The Final Countdown* has not been to set dates. <u>Its main purpose has been to reveal that Daniel's prophecy has a *Final Decree* that everyone missed, and it is about to be fulfilled.</u> As outlined in the **Preface**, the wise and faithful servant will know the time when the Lord returns and not be taken by surprise. The Second Fulfillment of Daniel's Seventy Weeks is almost finished. What if this book is not a false alarm?

Appendix 4 – Abraham Accords

Ever since Joe Biden took office we have witnessed his administration dismantling many of the major accomplishments that President Donald J. Trump achieved. The one major feature Joe Biden did not destroy was the important Abraham Accords. On the contrary, he actually welcomed the Accords and in his trip in July 2022, he even commended Saudi Arabia's recent historic decision of lifting the restrictions on all air carriers from using its airspace.

One of the major (behind the scenes) architects of the Abraham Accords was Jared Kushner who was President Donald J. Trump's key draftsman and negotiator. His talents as President Trump's senior advisor helped broker four historic peace agreements that prior Presidents were unable to achieve. His successful negotiation of the Abraham Accords was the most significant diplomatic breakthrough in fifty years and earned him a nomination for the Nobel Peace Prize.

In Jared Kushner's recent book: **Breaking History** he provides us with distinctive evidence that God's hand was at work in bringing together several of Israel's neighbors to the peace table. 2020 was a momentous year when the course of history was changed. Kushner's enthralling account provides us with a clear demonstration of God's divine hand as He intervened in history. The important peace accords that were made with many nations marked 2020 as the start of the final 70th Week in the Second Fulfillment of Daniel's Seventy Weeks prophecy. These covenants occurred 483 years (69 Weeks x 7) after Sultan Suleiman's decree in 1537. The final Seven Years began in 2020, with the signing of these notable peace covenants.

If anyone has any doubts about this or thinks that this book is another false alarm, they should read Jared Kushner's remarkable book. God's hand was clearly at work in fashioning the peace covenants outlined in the Abraham Accords.

Year of Jubilee

There are at least two references in Scripture that point us to Jubilee Years. The first one was found by rabbis who connected Ezekiel 40:1 with Leviticus 25:9-10. As noted by Dr. Widener: "The Talmud records their opinion that the twenty-fifth year after the first exile there was a jubilee year, because only in the Year of Jubilee does the New Year (Rosh Hashanah) begin on the tenth of Tishri...with the date of the first exile beginning on 2 Adar 597 BC, there was a Year of Jubilee that began on 10 Tishri 574 BC in the twenty-fifth year of their exile (Ezekiel 40:1)." (Widener, pp. 265-266)

The other Scripture that describes a Jubilee Year was when Jesus began His ministry and He visited a synagogue on the Sabbath where He read from the scroll of Isaiah. This was recorded for us by Luke:

*The Spirit of the Lord is on me, because he has anointed me to proclaim good news to the poor, He has sent me to proclaim **freedom for the prisoners** and recovery of sight for the blind, **to set the oppressed free**, to proclaim **the year of the Lord's favor**.*
(Luke 4:18-19)

Jesus then stopped reading and said, "*Today, this Scripture is fulfilled in your hearing.*" What He had just read included proclaiming the Year of the Lord's favor (which means a **Year of Jubilee**), which He said was just fulfilled. From this, we can conclude that when Jesus began His ministry in AD 27, He proclaimed that it was a Jubilee Year.

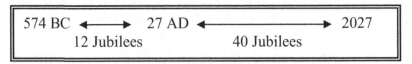

By connecting these two Jubilee Years (574 BC and 27 AD) we can extrapolate 40 Jubilees (40 x 50 = 2,000 years), which takes us to the Jubilee Year in 2027. Remember that **Jesus** spent 40 days in the wilderness after He was baptized, and the **Israelites** wandered in the wilderness for 40 years. Are these foreshadowing Jesus would provide for 40 Jubilees – one Jubilee for each day that He spent in the wilderness? And, as believers, aren't we just **pilgrims** in the wilderness on the earth (for a period of 40 Jubilees) looking for our heavenly city? (Hebrews 11:13-16, 1 Peter 2:9-11) Even so, come Lord Jesus!

Appendix 5 – Signs of Christ's Coming

Many modern Bible teachers and students believe that the rebirth of the nation of Israel represents the budding of the *fig tree* that Jesus described to His disciples as He sat on the Mount of Olives, and we are living in the generation that won't pass away before He returns.

Verily I say unto you, this generation shall not pass,
till all these things be fulfilled. (Matthew 24:34 – KJV)

With Israel becoming a nation in 1948, we have been alerted that the Lord's return is fast approaching. Jesus also told his disciples a second sign to look for in the parable of Noah:

As it was in the days of Noah,
so it will be at the coming of the Son of Man.
(Matthew 24:37 – NIV)

Here the Lord is telling the Church that just before His return, things will be the same as they were back in Noah's day. This pictures life going on right up until the day that the rapture occurs, and the judgments of God are suddenly released upon the earth. A careful study of Genesis 6 will alert the reader to the fact that living in these end times is almost parallel to the time before the flood. The world has become a great cesspool of corruption, violence, sex, drugs, idolatry, witchcraft and other perversions. Reading the account in Genesis is like reading today's newspaper or listening to the daily news.

In the Lord's parable concerning Noah, Jesus was also giving us a second important sign that His return is drawing very near. Several years ago a famous comet passed through our solar system and it was hailed as the most-watched comet of all time.

April 8, 1997

Comet Hale-Bopp Over New York City
Credit and Copyright: J. Sivo
http://antwrp.gsfc.nasa.gov/apod/ap970408.html

"What's that point of light above the World Trade Center? It's Comet Hale-Bopp! Both faster than a speeding bullet and able to "leap" tall buildings in its single orbit, Comet Hale-Bopp is also bright enough to be seen even over the glowing lights of one of the world's premier cities. In the foreground lies the East River, while much of New York City's Lower Manhattan can be seen between the river and the comet."

As it was in the days of Noah,
so it will be at the coming of the Son of Man.
(Matthew 24:37 – NIV)

These words from our wonderful Lord have several applications about the Tribulation period that is about to ensnare this world.

Seas Lifted Up

Throughout the Old Testament, the time of the coming Tribulation period is described as the time when the "seas have lifted up," and also as coming in as a "flood" (please see Jeremiah 51:42, Hosea 5:10, Daniel 11:40 and Psalm 93:3-4 for just a few examples).

This is a direct parallel to the time of Noah when the Great Flood of water came to wipe out every living creature except for righteous Noah and his family, and the pairs of animals God spared. While God said He would never flood the earth again with water, the coming Judgement will be by fire (II Peter 3:10). The book of Revelation shows that approximately three billion people will perish in the terrible time that lies ahead (see Revelation 6:8 and 9:15).

2 Witnesses

A guiding principle of God is to establish a matter based upon the witness of two or more:

> ...a matter must be established by the testimony of two or three witnesses (Deuteronomy 19:15 – NIV)

In 1994, God was able to get the attention of mankind when Comet Shoemaker-Levy crashed into Jupiter on the 9th of Av (on the Jewish calendar). Interestingly, this Comet was named after the "two" witnesses who first discovered it.

In 1995, "two" more astronomers also discovered another comet. It was called Comet Hale-Bopp, and it reached its closest approach to planet Earth on March 23, 1997. It has been labeled as the most widely viewed comet in the history of mankind.

Scientists have determined that Comet Hale-Bopp's orbit brought it to our solar system 4,465 years ago (see Notes 1 and 2 below). In other words, the comet made its appearance near Earth in 1997 and also in 2468 BC. Remarkably, this comet preceded the Great Flood by 120 years! God warned Noah of this in Genesis 6:3:

> My Spirit shall not strive with man forever, for he is indeed flesh; yet his days shall be one hundred and twenty years.

Days of Noah

What does all of this have to do with the Lord's return? Noah was born around 2948 BC, and Genesis 7:11 tells us that the Flood took place when Noah was 600, or in 2348 BC.

Remember, our Lord told us: *"As it was in the days of Noah, so it will be at the coming of the Son of Man.* (Matthew 24:37 – NIV)

In the original Greek, it is saying: *"exactly like"* it was, so it will be when He comes (see Strong's #5618).

During the days of Noah, Comet Hale-Bopp arrived on the scene as a harbinger of the Great Flood. Just as this same comet appeared before the Flood, could its arrival again in 1997 be a sign that God's final Judgement, also known as the time of Jacob's Trouble, is about to begin?

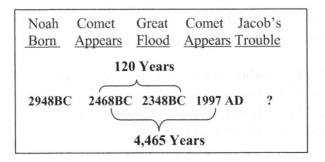

Comet Hale-Bopp arrived 120 years before the Flood as a warning to mankind. Only righteous Noah heeded God's warning and built the ark, as God instructed. By faith, Noah was obedient to God and, as a result, saved himself and his family from destruction.

Remember, Jesus told us His return would be preceded by great heavenly signs: *"And there shall be signs in the sun, and in the moon, and in the stars; and upon the earth distress of nations, with perplexity; the sea and the waves roaring..."* (Luke 21:25)

Jesus was asked 3 questions by the disciples:
"Tell us, (1) when shall these things be" (the destruction of the city of Jerusalem), *" and (2) what shall be the **sign** of thy coming, and (3) of the end of the world?"* (Matthew 24:3)

Just as this large comet appeared as a 120-year warning to Noah, its arrival in 1997 tells us that Jesus is getting ready to return again. Is this the **"Sign"** Jesus referred to?

Sign of Christ's Coming

The **first** question had to do with events that were fulfilled in 70 AD. The **third** question has to do with the future time at the very end of the age.

The **second** question, however, has to do with the time of Christ's second coming. Jesus answered this second question in His description of the days of Noah found in Matthew 24:33-39:

> *[37] But as the days of Noe were, so shall also the coming of the Son of man be. [38]For as in the days that were before the flood they were eating and drinking, marrying and giving in marriage, until the day that Noe entered into the ark, [39] And knew not until the flood came, and took them all away; so shall also the coming of the Son of man be.*

Jesus is telling us that the **_sign_** of His coming will be as it was during the days of Noah. As Comet Hale-Bopp was a sign to the people in Noah's day, its arrival in 1997 is a sign that Jesus is coming back again soon. Comet Hale-Bopp could be the very sign Jesus was referring to, which would announce His return for His faithful.

Remember, Jesus said, *"**exactly as** it was in the days of Noah, so will it be when He returns."* The appearance of Comet Hale-Bopp in 1997 is a strong indication that the Tribulation period is about to begin, but before then, Jesus is coming for His bride!

Keep looking up! Jesus is coming again very soon!

As Noah prepared for the destruction God warned him about 120 years before the Flood, Jesus has given mankind a final warning that the Tribulation period is about to begin. The horrible destruction on 9/11 is only a precursor of what is about to take place on planet Earth. We need to be wise like Noah and prepare. Always remember our Lord's instructions in Luke 21:34-36:

> *(34)And take heed to yourselves, lest at any time your hearts be overcharged with surfeiting, and drunkenness, and cares of this life, and so that day come upon you unawares. (35) For as a snare shall it come on all them that dwell on the face of the whole earth. (36)**Watch ye therefore, and _pray always_, that ye may be _accounted worthy to escape_ all these things that shall come to pass, and to stand before the Son of man*** (Luke 21:34-36).

Footnotes to Appendix 5

(1) The original orbit of Comet Hale-Bopp was calculated to be approximately 265 years by engineer George Sanctuary in his article, *Three Craters In Israel*, published on 3/31/01 found in the Supplemental Articles for *Coming Spiritual Earthquake*.

Comet Hale-Bopp's orbit around the time of the Flood changed from 265 years to about 4,200 years. Because the plane of the comet's orbit is perpendicular to the earth's orbital plane (ecliptic), Mr. Sanctuary noted: "A negative time increment was used for this simulation...to back the comet away from the earth.... past Jupiter... and then out of the solar system. The simulation suggests that the past-past orbit had a very eccentric orbit with a period of only 265 years. When the comet passed Jupiter (*around 2203BC*) its orbit was deflected upward, coming down near the earth 15 months later with the comet's period changed from 265 years to about (*4,200*) years." (*added text for clarity*)

(2) Don Yeomans, with NASA's Jet Propulsion Laboratory, made the following observations regarding the comet's orbit: "By integrating the above orbit forward and backward in time until the comet leaves the planetary system and then referring the osculating orbital elements...the following orbital periods result: Original orbital period before entering planetary system = 4200 years. Future orbital period after exiting the planetary system = 2380 years."

This analysis can be found at:

http://www2.jpl.nasa.gov/comet/ephemjpl6.html

Based upon the above two calculations we have the following:

265 [a] + 4,200 [b] = 4,465 Years

1997 AD – 4,465 Years = 2468 BC = Hale Bopp arrived

(a) Orbit period calculated by George Sanctuary before deflection around 2203 BC.

(b) Orbit period calculated by Don Yeomans after 1997 visit.

Tract Included In Appendix 5

This tract was written in 1997 when Comet Hale-Bopp entered our solar system. In 2027 it will be the 30th Anniversary of its last appearance. Bullinger wrote, "30, being 3x10 denotes in a higher degree the perfection of Divine order, as marking the **right moment**. Christ was thirty years of age at the commencement of His ministry. David was also 30 when he began to reign." (Bullinger, p. 265). Was Comet Hale-Bopp giving us a sign that the bride of Christ is about to begin her reign and Christ will return in 2027? **Is this further corroboration that 2027 will be the time for Christ's Second Coming?** (See Ezekiel 33:1-6).

Special Invitation

This book was primarily written for those who have been born again. If you have never been born again, would you like to be? The Bible shows that it's simple to be saved...

- **Realize you are a sinner.**
  "As it is written, There is none righteous, no, not one:"
  (Romans 3:10)
  "... for there is no difference. For all have sinned, and come short of the glory of God;" (Romans 3:22-23)

- **Realize you CAN NOT save yourself.**
  "But we are all as an unclean thing, and all our righteousness are as filthy rags; ..." (Isaiah 64:6)
  "Not by works of righteousness which we have done, but according to his mercy he saved us, ..." (Titus 3:5)

- **Realize that Jesus Christ died on the cross to pay for your sins.**
  "Who his own self bare our sins in his own body on the tree,..."
  (I Peter 2:24)
  "... Unto him that loved us, and washed us from our sins in his own blood," (Revelation 1:5)

- **Simply by faith receive Jesus Christ as your personal Savior.**
  "But as many as received him, to them gave he power to become the sons of God, even to them that believe on his name:" (John 1:12)
  " ...Sirs, what must I do to be saved? And they said, Believe on the Lord Jesus Christ, and thou shalt be saved, and thy house."
  (Acts 16:30-31)

WOULD YOU LIKE TO BE SAVED?

If you would like to be saved, believe on the Lord Jesus Christ right now by making this acknowledgment in your heart:

> Lord Jesus, I know that I am a sinner, and unless You save me, I am lost forever. I thank You for dying for me at Calvary. By faith I come to You now, Lord, the best way I know how, and ask You to save me. I believe that God raised You from the dead and acknowledge You as my personal Saviour.

If you believed on the Lord, this is the most important decision of your life. You are now saved by the precious blood of Jesus Christ, which was shed for you and your sins. Now that you have believed on Jesus as your personal Saviour, you will want to find a Church where you can be baptized as your first act of obedience, and where the Word of God is taught so you can continue to grow in your faith. Ask the Holy Spirit to help you as you read the Bible to learn all that God has for your life.

Also, please see the Bibliography, as well as the pages that follow for information on several books that will help you on your wonderful journey and help you prepare for the days ahead.

Endtimes

The Bible indicates that we are living in the final days and Jesus Christ is getting ready to return very soon. This book was written to help Christians prepare for what lies ahead. The Word of God indicates that the Tribulation Period is rapidly approaching and that the Antichrist is getting ready to emerge on the world scene.

Jesus promised His disciples that there is a way to escape the horrible time of testing and persecution that will soon devastate this planet. The main purpose of this book is to help you get prepared so you will rule and reign with Jesus when He returns.

About The Author

Jim Harman has been a Christian for more than 44 years. He has diligently studied the Word of God with a particular emphasis on Prophecy. Jim has written several books and the most essential titles are available at www.ProphecyCountdown.com: *The Coming Spiritual Earthquake, The Kingdom, Overcomers' Guide To The Kingdom, Calling All Overcomers, Come Away My Beloved, Daniel's Prophecies Unsealed, and Salvation of the Soul;* which have been widely distributed around the world. These books will encourage you to continue *"Looking"* for the Lord's soon return.

Jim's professional experience included being a Certified Public Accountant (CPA) and a Certified Property Manager (CPM). He had an extensive background in both public accounting and financial management with several well-known national firms.

Jim was fortunate to have been acquainted with several mature believers who understand and teach the deeper truths of the Bible. It is Jim's strong desire that many will come to realize the vital importance of seeking the Kingdom and seeking Christ's righteousness as we approach the soon return of our Lord and Saviour Jesus Christ.

The burden of Jim's heart is to see many believers come to know the joy of Christ's triumph in their life as they become true overcomers; qualified and ready to rule and reign with Christ in the coming Kingdom.

To contact Jim for questions, to arrange for speaking engagements, or to order multiple copies of his books:

Jim Harman
P.O. Box 941612
Maitland, FL 32794
JimHarmanCPA@gmail.com

Final Thoughts

If the analysis in this book is correct then the Second Coming of Christ will take place in 2027. This computation is based upon Dr. Widener's discovery of the decree made by Sultan Suleiman in 1537. Since he restored Jerusalem between 1537-1541, it is possible that the start date for the initial decree may be off by a year or so.

In the Afterword to his book, *Witnessing The End*, Dr. Widener cautions us: "Because of the timeliness of events, the 2020-2027 window is even now being tested. We won't know for certain if all these things really mean we are at the end until we get there, but I wouldn't be much of a watchman if I waited until the enemy was at the gates to sound the alarm....I think the world has reached the point that I can call someone else to the wall and ask them to gaze out into the mist and the distance and tell me if they too see the approaching enemy, and they will say, 'Yes! Sound the alarm!'" Rest assured that God will fulfill His Word exactly as he has declared and planned, from before the foundation of the world, at exactly the right time (Widener, pp. 407-408)

When I discovered Dr. Widener's shocking new discovery, I immediately felt that the Lord had called me to join him in sounding the alarm. Could it be wrong? Yes, of course, it could be; however, the best evidence points to 1537 because of other corroborating evidence Dr. Widener gives in his book, particularly his case for the Jubilee cycle ending in 2027. In addition, Jared Kushner's recent book: *Breaking History* presents valuable evidence that the peace covenants made with many nations crucially marked 2020, as the start of the final 70th Week in the Second Fulfillment of Daniel's Seventy Weeks. Keep looking UP! Jesus is coming very soon. Make sure that you are ready and make sure all of your friends and loved ones that you care about are prepared for what is about to take place.

The end of the world is coming soon.
Therefore be earnest,
Thoughtful men of prayer.
(1 Peter 4:7 – Paraphrase)

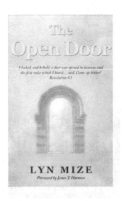

The Open Door was written to reveal the Scriptures that will help you learn how to watch for, and be a part of Jesus Christ's coming Kingdom. If you are seeking more than simple answers, this book will show you the deeper truths in the Scriptures that will lead you to a closeness with Christ now, and a position with Him in His coming Kingdom in the very near future.

The message in this timely prophetic book will help you understand:

- The Judgment Seat Christ will not be an award ceremony for every Christian.
- Which one of the Seven Feasts the Rapture will occur on.
- How you can obtain the 5 Crowns mentioned in the Bible.
- How you can ensure you will be part of the Bride of Christ.
- What the Seven Parables of the Kingdom really mean.
- Which of the Seven Churches you should be a member in.
- The future destiny of the United States of America.
- The startling identity of the Antichrist who is about to emerge.
- How you can escape the coming tribulation period.
- How you can reign and rule with the King of the Universe.

Jesus went away almost 2,000 years ago and He is in the process of preparing a Holy City for all overcoming believers. Lyn Mize has given us an excellent resource that can be instrumental in helping us qualify to become part of those who will reign and rule with Jesus in this magnificent Holy City.

Available From Amazon.com

Paperback, *Kindle* and *Audible* Editions

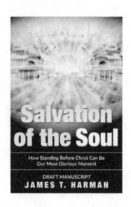

HOW STANDING BEFORE CHRIST
CAN BE OUR MOST GLORIOUS MOMENT

The topic of the Judgment Seat of Christ is often neglected by today's modern church.

> *"For we must all appear before the judgment seat of Christ, that each one may receive the things done in the body, according to what he has done, whether good or bad"* (2 Corinthians 5:10).

When Jesus returns, He will review all of our lives to determine whether we have been faithful and obedient doers of His Word. The purpose of this book is to prepare believers so they will be able to hear Him say:

> *"Well done, good and faithful servant....*
> ***Enter into the joy of your lord"*** (Matthew 25:21).

MUST-READ FOR ALL BELIEVERS

NEW DISCOVERY – LEARN ABOUT
- Difference between the salvation of spirit and soul.
- What Jesus meant by *"take up your cross."*
- How the Word of God can save our souls.
- When the salvation of our soul takes place.
- Sign of Christ's Coming

Download your FREE copy: www.ProphecyCountdown.com

Order your copy today ***Paperback – eBook – Audio*** Editions

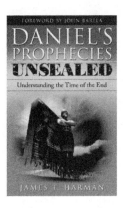

"Go your way Daniel, because the words are closed up and sealed until the time of the end...none of the wicked will understand, but those who are wise will understand."
(Daniel 12:9-10)

The Archangel Michael told Daniel that the prophecies would be sealed until the time of the end. Discover how the prophecies in the book of Daniel are being unsealed in the events taking place today.

Since Daniel was told that the wise will understand the message and lead many to righteousness, while the wicked will not grasp its meaning and will continue in their wickedness, it is imperative for everyone living in these end times to diligently examine and attempt to comprehend the vital message Daniel has recorded for us. The wise will diligently search the word of the Lord and ask for wisdom in order to understand God's plan.

When Jesus came the first time, the wise men of the day were aware of His soon arrival and they were actively looking for Him. Today, those who are wise will be passionately sharing this message and helping others prepare. Those doing so will *"shine like the stars forever and ever."*

May the Lord grant us a heart of wisdom to understand the time we are living in so we can prepare for what lies ahead!

Download your FREE copy: www.ProphecyCountdown.com

Order your copy today: ***Paperback – eBook – Audio*** Editions

God placed the ***Song of Solomon*** in the heart of the Bible for a special reason. ***Come Away My Beloved*** helps reveal that reason in a most enchanting way. In this refreshing commentary, you will realize why this ancient love story has perplexed Bible students and commentators down through the ages.

Find out the prophetic importance veiled within the Song's poetic imagery and experience a renewed love for the Lord as you explore one of the most passionate love stories of all time.

Witness the wonderful joys of romance and devotion shared by two young lovers. Discover enduring lessons of virtue and faithfulness, and learn amazing truths that have been hidden within the greatest love Song ever written.

Written almost 3,000 years ago this brilliant Song of love reflects God's desire for every man and woman; not only in their present lives but also in their relationship with Him.

This book will revive your heart with a fervent love for your Saviour. It will also help you prepare for your glorious wedding day when Jesus returns for His devoted bride.

Allow this beautiful story of love and passion to ignite a flame in your heart and let this inspirational Song arouse your heart to join in the impassioned cry with the rest of the bride:

"Make haste, my beloved, and come quickly…"
Download your FREE copy: www.ProphecyCountdown.com

Order your copy today: ***Paperback – eBook*** Editions

Perplexed by the book of Revelation? Not sure what all the signs, symbols and metaphors really mean? Jim Harman's latest work unravels Apostle John's remarkable revelation of Jesus Christ and what's in store for the inhabitants of planet Earth. This extraordinary commentary is not another cookie-cutter rehash of the popular teachings fostered by the *Left Behind* phenomena so prevalent in today's church.

One of the central messages in the book of Revelation is that God is calling men to be genuine overcomers. Jesus Christ has been sent out from the throne of God to conquer men's hearts so they can also be overcomers.

The purpose of this book is to encourage people to embrace Him as the King of their hearts and allow His life to reign in theirs. He wants you to be able to overcome by His mighty power and strength living inside of you just as He overcame for all of us. Jesus will be looking for a faithful remnant qualified to rule and reign with Him when He returns. This book will help you prepare to be the overcomer for which Jesus is looking.

The reader will come away with a new and enlightened understanding of what the last book in God's Word is all about. Understand the book of Revelation and why it is so important for believers living in the last days of the Church age.

Download your FREE copy: www.ProphecyCountdown.com

Order your copy today: *Paperback – eBook* Editions

Once a person is saved, the number one priority should be seeking entrance into the Kingdom through the salvation of their soul. It is pictured as a runner in a race seeking a prize represented by a crown that will last forever.

The salvation of the soul and entrance into the coming Kingdom are only achieved through much testing and the trial of one's faith. If you are going through difficulty, then REJOICE:

> *"Blessed is the man who perseveres under trial, because when he has stood the test, he will receive the crown of life that God has promised to those who love Him."* (James 1:12)

The "Traditional" teaching on the "THE KINGDOM" has taken the Church captive into believing all Christians will rule and reign with Christ no matter if they have lived faithful and obedient lives, or if they have been slothful and disobedient with the talents God has given them. Find out the important Truth before Jesus Christ returns.

MUST READING FOR EVERY CHRISTIAN

Jesus Christ is returning for His faithful overcoming followers. Don't miss the opportunity of ruling and reigning with Christ in the coming KINGDOM!

Download your FREE copy: www.ProphecyCountdown.com

Order your copy today: *Paperback – eBook* Editions

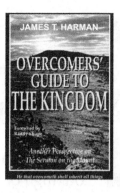

Get ready to climb back up the Mountain to listen to Christ's teachings once again. Though you may have read His great *Sermon on the Mount* many times, discover exciting promises that many have missed.

The purpose of this book is to help Christians be the Overcomers Jesus wants them to be and to help them gain their own entrance in the coming Kingdom. Learn what seeking the Kingdom of God is all about and be among the chosen few who will "enter into" the coming Kingdom. *"Whoever hears these sayings of Mine, and does them, I will liken him to a wise man who built his house upon the rock."* (Matthew 7:24)

Also, learn about:
- The link between Beatitudes and Fruit of the Spirit
- What the "law of Christ" really is
- The critical importance of the "Lord's prayer"
- How to be an Overcomer
- THE SIGN of Christ's soon Coming
- A new song entitled: LOOKING FOR THE SON which has the message of how vitally important it is to be Watching for the Lord's return and the consequences to those who are not looking.

Download your FREE copy: www.ProphecyCountdown.com

Order your copy today: *Paperback – eBook – Audio* Editions

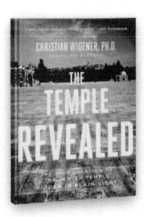

LOOKING FOR THE SON
Lyrics by Jim Harman
Listen to this Song on the Home Page of Prophecy Countdown

Lyric	Scripture
There's a fire burning in my heart	Luke 24:32
Yearning for the Lord to come,	Rev. 22:17, Mat. 6:33
and His Kingdom come to start	
Soon He'll come.....so enter the narrow gate	Lk. 21:34-36,Mat.7:13
Even though you mock me now...	II Peter 3:4
He'll come to set things straight	
Watch how I'll leave in the twinkling of an eye	I Corinthians 15:52
Don't be surprised when I go up in the sky	Revelation 3:10
There's a fire burning in my heart	Luke 24:32
Yearning for my precious Lord	Revelation 22:17
And His Kingdom come to start	Revelation 20:4-6
Your love of this world, has forsaken His	I John 2:15
It leaves me knowing that you could have had it all	Revelation 21:7
Your love of this world, was oh so reckless	Revelation 3:14-22
I can't help thinking	Philippians 1:3-6
You would have had it all	Revelation 21:7
Looking for the Son	Titus 2:13, Luke 21:36
(Tears are gonna fall, not looking for the Son)	Matthew 25:10-13
You had His holy Word in your hand	II Timothy 3:16
(You're gonna wish you had listened to me)	Jeremiah 25:4-8
And you missed it...for your self	Matthew 22:11-14
(Tears are gonna fall, not looking for the Son)	Matthew 25:10-13
Brother, I have a story to be told	Habakkuk 2:2
It's the only one that's true	John 3:16-17
And it should've made your heart turn	II Peter 3:9
Remember me when I rise up in the air	I Corinthians 15:52
Leaving your home down here	I Corinthians 15:52
For true Treasures beyond compare	Matthew 6:20
Your love of this world, has forsaken His	I John 2:15
It leaves me knowing that you could have had it all	Revelation 21:7
Your love of this world, was oh so reckless	Revelation 3:14-22
I can't help thinking	Philippians 1:3-6
You would have had it all	Revelation 21:7

(Lyrics in parentheses represent background vocals)

(CONTINUED)

Lyric	Scripture
Looking for the Son	Titus 2:13, Lk. 21:36
(Tears are gonna fall, not looking for the Son)	Matthew 25:10-13
You had His holy Word in your hand	II Timothy 3:16
(You're gonna wish you had listened to me)	Jeremiah 25:4-8
And you lost it...for your self	Matthew 22:11-14
(Tears are gonna fall, not looking for the Son)	Matthew 25:10-13
You would have had it all	Revelation 21:7
Looking for the Son	Titus 2:13, Lk. 21:36
You had His holy Word in your hand	II Timothy 3:16
But you missed it... for your self	Matthew 22:11-14
Lov'n the world....not the open door	I Jn. 2:15, Rev. 4:1
Down the broad way... blind to what life's really for	Matthew 7:13-14
Turn around now...while there still is time	I Jn. 1:9, II Pet. 3:9
Learn your lesson now or you'll reap just what you sow	Galatians 6:7

(You're gonna wish you had listened to me)
You would have had it all
(Tears are gonna fall, not looking for the Son)
You would have had it all
(You're gonna wish you had listened to me)
It all, it all, it all
(Tears are gonna fall, not looking for the Son)

You would have had it all
(You're gonna wish you had listened to me)
Looking for the Son
(Tears are gonna fall, not looking for the Son)
You had His holy Word in your hand
(You're gonna wish you had listened to me)
And you missed it...for yourself
(Tears are gonna fall, not looking for the Son)

You would have had it all
(You're gonna wish you had listened to me)
Looking for the Son
(Tears are gonna fall, not looking for the Son)
You had His holy Word in your hand
(You're gonna wish you had listened to me)
But you missed it
You missed it
You missed it
You missed it....for yourself

Scripture Summary
Jeremiah 25:4-8
Habakkuk 2:2
Matthew 6:20
Matthew 6:33
Matthew 7:13
Matthew 22:11-14
Matthew 25:10-13
Luke 21:34-36
Luke 24:332
John 3:16-17
I Corinthians 15:52
Galatians 6:7
Philippians 1:3-6
II Timothy 3:16
Titus 2:13
II Peter 3:9
II Peter 3:4
I John 1:9
I John 2:15
Revelation 3:10
Revelation 3:14-22
Revelation 4:1
Revelation 20:4-6
Revelation 21:7
Revelation 22:17

(See www.ProphecyCountdown.com for more information)

The Day of the Lord is Near!

The Coming Spiritual Earthquake

by James T. Harman

"The Message presented in this book is greatly needed to awaken believers to the false ideas many have when it comes to the Rapture. I might have titled it: THE RAPTURE EARTH-QUAKE!"
Ray Brubaker - God's News Behind the News

"If I am wrong, anyone who follows the directions given in this book will be better off spiritually. If I am right, they will be among the few to escape the great-est spiritual calamity of the ages."
Jim Harman - Author

**MUST READING FOR EVERY CHRISTIAN!
HURRY! BEFORE IT IS TOO LATE!**

Made in the USA
Coppell, TX
03 May 2024

31983527R00056